The Poetic World of Boris Pasternak

The Poetic World of
Boris Pasternak

OLGA R. HUGHES

Princeton University Press

Library of Congress Cataloging in Publication Data
will be found on the last printed page of this book

Publication of this book has been aided by a grant
from the Andrew W. Mellon Foundation

Printed in the United States of America
by Princeton University Press,
Princeton, New Jersey

For my Father and Mother

NOTE ON TRANSLITERATION

QUOTATIONS from Pasternak's verse are given in the original followed by a prose translation. Anything in prose—fictional, autobiographical, critical, or epistolary—is given in translation only. Translations, except as noted, are mine.

In the notes and Bibliography the system of Transliteration employed by Slavic scholars was used.

ACKNOWLEDGMENTS

I WISH TO thank for his encouragement, advice and help Professor Gleb Struve, whose great knowledge and love of Pasternak's work, as well as his extraordinary generosity in sharing those materials in his possession which were not generally available, were of incalculable help; Professor Simon Karlinsky for his careful reading of the first draft and for valuable suggestions at various stages of my work; and Professor Nicholas Riasanovsky for his general criticism and discussion of individual chapters that helped to improve many sections of this work.

I am very grateful to Professor Francis J. Whitfield for reading the manuscript in its entirety and suggesting numerous stylistic improvements.

In addition, I wish to thank Mrs. Beatrice Nosco for permission to quote Pasternak's letter to her, and Professor George Myro for obtaining for me copies of those of Pasternak's published letters which are not available in the libraries of the West Coast.

I thank Robert P. Hughes for encouraging me to undertake a study of Boris Pasternak, for helping me in the course of my work in more ways than can be enumerated, and for his infinite patience in going over the text and especially over my renditions of the quotations from Pasternak.

O. R. H.

Berkeley, California
November 1971

CHRONOLOGY

1890 Jan. 29 (Feb. 10)	born in Moscow
1903 summer	meets Alexander Skryabin for the first time; begins serious study of music
1906	travels to Berlin with his family
1909	abandons study of music; enters the University of Moscow
1912	summer semester at the University of Marburg; travels to Italy
1913	graduates from the University of Moscow; first poems published
1914	takes part in a futurist group, Centrifuge; meets Vladimir Mayakovsky; *A Twin in the Clouds* (first book of verse) published
1915–1916 and 1916–1917 } winters	works and travels in the Urals
1917 March	returns to Moscow; *Above the Barriers* (a book of verse)
1918	"Apelles' Mark," first story in prose
1922	begins correspondence with Marina Tsvetaeva; travels to Berlin and Marburg; *My Sister, Life (Summer 1917)* (a book of verse); stories "Childhood of Luvers" and "Letters from Tula"

CHRONOLOGY

1923	*Themes and Variations* (a book of verse)
1924	"Lofty Malady" (a longer poem); "Aerial Ways" (a story)
1927	longer poems "The Year 1905" and "Lieutenant Schmidt"
1929	*A Tale* (a story)
1930	Vladimir Mayakovsky's suicide
1931	travels for the first time to Georgia; beginning of the friendship with Paolo Yashvili, Titian and Nina Tabidze, Simon Chikovani; *Spektorsky* (a novel in verse); *Safe Conduct* (an autobiographical essay)
1932	*Second Birth* (a book of verse)
1933 Nov.	a trip to Georgia with a group of writers
1934	participates in the First All-Union Congress of Soviet Writers; Nikolai Bukharin's speech at the Congress draws special attention to Pasternak; moves to Peredelkino
1935 June	takes part in the International Writers' Congress in Paris as an official representative of Soviet Writers' Union; *Georgian Lyric Poets* (translations from the Georgian)
1937	suicide of Paolo Yashvili; arrest of Titian Tabidze
1940	*Selected Translations* (Kleist, Shakespeare, Raleigh, Byron, Keats, Petöfi, Verlaine, Becher, Hans Sachs)
1941	Marina Tsvetaeva's suicide; translation of "Hamlet"
1941–1942 and 1942–1943 } winters	stays with his family in Chistopol on the Kama
1943 August	a trip to the front with a group of writers; *On Early Trains* (a book of verse)

xii

1945	*Terrestrial Expanse* (a book of verse)
1949	*William Shakespeare in Boris Pasternak's Translation* (2 volumes)
1953	translation of Goethe's *Faust*
1954	ten poems from *Doctor Zhivago* published in *Znamya* (Moscow)
1956	*Doctor Zhivago* rejected by the editorial board of *Novy Mir* (letter of rejection published only on Oct. 25, 1958)
1957	*Doctor Zhivago* published in Italy
1958	*Poems about Georgia. Georgian Poets* (published in Tbilisi); translation of Schiller's "Maria Stuart"; begins work on dramatic trilogy *A Blind Beauty* (only a draft of the prologue remains)
Oct. 23	awarded Nobel prize for literature
Oct. 27	expelled from the Union of Soviet Writers
1959 Feb.	last trip to Georgia
June	*When the Weather Clears* (last book of verse) published in Paris
1960 May 30	dies in Peredelkino

TABLE OF CONTENTS

The Poetic World of Boris Pasternak

"Другие по живому следу
Пройдут твой путь за пядью пядь."
(*Сочинения*, III, 63)
"*On your fresh track, others
Will follow your path step by step.*"

INTRODUCTION

IN HIS predilection for paradoxical statements, Boris Pasternak once declared that "aesthetics does not exist."[1] In the poet's opinion, formal aesthetics deserves such categorical rejection for being divorced from reality, for knowing nothing about man, and for operating with abstract classifications. On another occasion and in a less paradoxical mood, Pasternak gave a concise definition of his understanding of what constitutes the "aesthetics of an artist." The three elements pointed out in this definition are the artist's conception of the nature of art, of the role of art in history, and of his own responsibility before history.[2] These two statements give a succinct characterization of Pasternak's approach to art. The artist's own views on art and their application in his work are important, rather than those "labels" which may be attached to him and his art in an attempt to assign him a place in a formal classification.

Next to nature and love, art itself is one of the permanent themes in Pasternak's work. The anonymous author of an article in *The Times Literary Supplement* referred to *Doctor Zhivago* as Pasternak's "Defence of Poesie": "*Doctor Zhivago*

---

[1] Boris Pasternak, *Sočinenija*, ed. Gleb Struve and Boris Filippov (Ann Arbor: The University of Michigan Press, 1961), III, 154. Unless otherwise stated, all subsequent references and quotations from Pasternak's works are to this edition. For designation of volumes, see Bibliography.

[2] *Sočinenija*, III, 160.

3

deals with the survival of poetry in catastrophic times. Since poetry counts no longer for most people as an activity of supreme value, Pasternak planned his novel as a Defence of Poesie."[3] The fact that Zhivago is a poet as well as a doctor serves as a realistic motivation for the discussion in the novel of the nature of art and poetic inspiration, of the relationship of art to life, and even of some technical aspects of a poet's work. These subjects were by no means new for the Pasternak of the forties and fifties. A poet, his vision of the world, and his relation to the surrounding life and society as well as to his art are not only major but constant themes of Pasternak's verse and prose. Careful reading forces one to see not only *Doctor Zhivago*, but the whole of Pasternak's work as a defense of poetry and to agree with the critic who sees his life and work as a "dissertation on art."[4]

Pasternak's first prose work "Апеллесова черта" ("Apelles' Mark," 1915) rather provocatively treats life itself as a creation of an artist. Both the narrator-protagonist of "Письма из Тулы" ("Letters from Tula," 1918) and the protagonist of *Повесть* (*A Tale*, 1929) are poets. The latter makes another appearance in the novel-in-verse *Spektorsky* (1924–1930). "Высокая болезнь" ("Lofty Malady," 1923, 1928) depicts an artist's response to the 1917 Revolution and to the revolutionary reality of the early 1920's. In his two autobiographies, *Охранная грамота* (*Safe Conduct*, 1929–1931) and *Автобиографический очерк* (*Autobiographical Sketch*, 1956), Pasternak speaks of those aspects of his early development and of the early influences which proved to be important for his art, describes the beginnings and the sources of his poetry, and presents his perception of the art of other poets.

Pasternak attached great importance to *Safe Conduct*. In *Autobiographical Sketch* he spoke of the discussion of his development in the earlier autobiography as being still valid

---

[3] "Zhivago's Defence," *The Times Literary Supplement*, March 11, 1965, pp. 185–86.

[4] Helen Muchnic, "Boris Pasternak and the Poems of Yurii Zhivago," *From Gorky to Pasternak* (New York: Random House, 1961), p. 397.

in the fifties.[5] Once he described it as "an honest and direct effort to understand ... what constitutes culture and art—if not in general, at least in the destiny of an individual man."[6]

Whether he is commenting on his own writing or on the problems of artistic translation, whether he is trying to define his position in contemporary Soviet literature or is interpreting the work of other writers, Pasternak almost always returns to the question of the origin of art in the life of the artist, its relation to life and reality, and the artist's position and role in contemporary society. The poet and his verses as a theme appear in Pasternak's lyric poetry, beginning with the poems of his first book of verse *Близнец в тучах* (*A Twin in the Clouds*, 1914). So the statement that Pasternak's life and work are a dissertation on art is not an exaggeration, and his work indeed can be interpreted as a defense of poetry. The title of his first autobiography, *Safe Conduct*, indicates that Pasternak's conscious aim in writing it was a justification of his course of action and an explanation of his position in Soviet literature and society. This purpose, undoubtedly, is most explicit in *Doctor Zhivago*.

There is an overwhelming and ever-present tendency in Pasternak's work to penetrate to the essential reality of life, whether it is in art, in human relations, or in history. His approach—which consciously avoids everything formal and scholastic—can be termed "existential" in the broadest sense of the term, as a concern with the fundamental problems of existence rather than with systems or ideologies. In his rejection of rigid categories and classifications, Pasternak is very consistent. Not only formal aesthetics is denied existence for losing touch with the reality of life; the protagonists of *Doctor Zhivago* consider formal philosophy as something superfluous and assign to it the role of a "seasoning" in art and life.[7]

---

[5] *Sočinenija*, II, 1.

[6] "Nine Letters of Boris Pasternak," *Harvard Library Bulletin*, XV, No. 4 (October 1967), pp. 317–30. These letters to Pasternak's translator George Reavey were translated and annotated by Elena Levin. The quotation appears on p. 320.

[7] *Sočinenija*, IV, 418.

INTRODUCTION

In this study, Pasternak's theoretical statements concerning art and the artist are used in conjunction with his metapoetry and the numerous depictions of the poet in verse and prose. This has proved a rewarding task, for not only is Pasternak consistent in his approach to life and art, but, despite some obvious changes that his poetry underwent in its chronological development, there is an all-pervading unity, especially strongly manifested in his views on art and on the role and the destiny of the poet.

No attempt is made here to reduce Pasternak's statements— scattered throughout his artistic, critical, autobiographical, and epistolary writings over a period of nearly fifty years—to any clear-cut system. Pasternak is allowed to speak for himself, and many of his remarks are paradoxical and cryptic, some ambiguous or contradictory. This fact, however, does not impair the underlying unity of his work, but rather emphasizes it by proving that the poet did not aim at theoretical or philosophical consistency. He never betrayed the only allegiance he did not tire of renewing—his allegiance to art.

CHAPTER ONE

The Origin and Nature of Poetry

"Я вышел на площадь. Я мог быть сочтен
Вторично родившимся. ..."
(Сочинения, I, 220)

*"I walked out onto the square. I could be regarded
As someone born for the second time."*

FOR PASTERNAK the nature of art is best revealed at the time
of its first appearance in the life of a creative artist—hence the
recurrence in his work of the theme of "the birth of a poet."

In the experience of the poet, the origin of art is most
closely connected with love and nature. Actually it is love—
which is identified with the energy of life—that brings about
the birth of the poet, who at this point suddenly perceives the
inherent ties between himself and nature.

The essence of life appears to the poet as a dynamic principle. Change is one of life's basic characteristics. It is experienced directly, but can be depicted by the means accessible
only to art.

THE ROAD TO POETRY

Pasternak published his first book of verse relatively late in
life. *A Twin in the Clouds* appeared in 1914, when the poet
was twenty-four. Most of the poems in the book were written
in the summer of the preceding year.[1] Yet in a poem written
in 1919 Pasternak places the birth of the poet in the child's
preconscious period of development. Pasternak's poet begins
his "life for verses and by means of verses"[2] very early. This
seeming discrepancy between the poem, which is a significant
statement on "the birth of a poet," and Pasternak's own

[1] *Sočinenija*, II, 31.
[2] *Ibid.*, I, 85.

7

biography is explained in both of his autobiographies: until the age of nineteen Pasternak devoted himself not to poetry but to music.

Pasternak attached a great significance to childhood and adolescence as the formative years that determine the essential characteristics of a person. He discussed the matter at some length in *Safe Conduct*.[3] In Pasternak's opinion, a distinct human personality is not granted as a free gift to all, but is created at a cost of sacrifices. Although everyone is eligible to become a unique individual, this potentiality is realized only to the extent to which the man himself is willing to contribute to the growth of his personality.

According to Pasternak, the response of an individual to the exceptional that he encounters in life does not simply reflect his limitations, but determines them. A majority of human beings turn out to be average only because they fear the sacrifices that life demands from those who choose uniqueness.

In a poem written in 1917, in complete accordance with these views, Pasternak proclaims every human soul an inexhaustible source of interest:

Как всякий факт на всяком бланке,
Так все дознанья хороши
О вакханалиях изнанки
Нескучного любой души.[4]

Just as every fact on every questionnaire is important,
So are all investigations
About the bacchanals of the inside,
Of the "never-a-dull-moment" of any soul.

In 1936 he defines a genius not only as related to ordinary men but as the best specimen of human race, its "immortal expression." In his opinion, there is no ordinary man who does not have an element of genius in him.[5] Doctor Zhivago speaks of all mothers as mothers of potentially great men.[6]

---

[3] *Ibid.*, II, 203–11.   [4] *Ibid.*, I, 87.
[5] *Ibid.*, III, 223.   [6] *Ibid.*, IV, 290.

Adolescence, in Pasternak's opinion, is an absolutely limitless region: it is the part that is greater than the whole; it serves as a permanent and inexhaustible source of memories, irrespective of the number of years an individual lives. Pasternak regarded his own childhood as the source of his inspiration and spiritual depth:

О детство! Ковш душевной глуби!
О всех лесов абориген,
Корнями вросший в самолюбье,
Мой вдохновитель, мой регент! (1917)[7]

O childhood! Vessel of spiritual depths!
Aborigine of all the forests,
Who is rooted firm in love of his self,
My inspiration and my ruler!

Adhering to his views on the role of the adolescent years in the life of an individual, Pasternak discusses in great detail those early influences in his life which he considered essential for his later development.

In both his autobiographies Pasternak mentions one particular night (November 23, 1894) when, as a four-year-old child, he was awakened by music. He singles out that night as the point after which his memory and consciousness began to function as in an adult. On that night the young boy, who by that time was used to the sound of piano music, was disturbed by the unfamiliar sounds of strings, which affected him as actual "cries for help and news of misfortune."[8]

The period of adolescence in Pasternak's life coincided with his serious interest in music and near-worship of Alexander Skryabin.[9] His first meeting with Skryabin took place in the summer of 1903, in Obolenskoe, where Pasternak listened to his father's conversations with the composer. Although he

[7] *Ibid.*, I, 83.

[8] *Ibid.*, II, 4.

[9] To Skrjabin and his influence are devoted several pages in *Oxrannaja gramota* (*Sočinenija*, II, 205–11) and a separate section in *Avtobiografičeskij očerk* (*Sočinenija*, II, 6–13).

often did not comprehend the essence of his views, Pasternak always sided with Skryabin, because, as he says, he was captured by the freshness of his spirit. Even before 1903 Pasternak had begun playing the piano and had attempted to write music; now under the influence of his admiration for Skryabin, he began a serious study of composition and devoted to it the next six years of his life.

Early in 1904 Skryabin left for Switzerland; it was five years later that Pasternak saw him again. Just as the meeting in the summer of 1903 determined Pasternak's development and interests for the six years that followed, so the 1909 encounter determined his future in general. He mentions that particular meeting as the turning point after which he gave up music entirely.

For Pasternak the significance of Skryabin himself greatly exceeded the importance of his music. In his own words, just as Dostoevsky was not only a novelist and Blok not only a poet, so Skryabin was not only a composer, but "the triumph incarnate ... of Russian culture."[10] Pasternak was not alone in his high appraisal of Skryabin, who was both a striking and at the same time typical representative of the Russian cultural renaissance of the early twentieth century. It was not Skryabin's music alone that led his contemporaries to form such a high opinion of him. Skryabin's personality and world view as expressed in his music helped to create the phenomenon of the man. It has been suggested that Skryabin's creative work was less interesting than his personality.[11] Soon after

[10] *Sočinenija*, II, 13.

[11] This is the view of Leonid Sabaneev, a music critic and composer, who knew Skrjabin personally, and spoke of his work as "a reflection of Russian literary symbolism in music" (Leonid Sabaneev, *Modern Russian Composers*, trans. from the Russian by Judah A. Joffe [New York: International Publishers, 1927], p. 44).

Richard Anthony Leonard, the author of a book on the history of Russian music, sees in the discrepancy between the artistic value of Skrjabin's music and the spiritual significance that he himself attached to it the source of his tragedy as an artist: "He was an artist of rare talent; his tastes were fine and his aspirations high; often he was boldly original.

Skryabin died, Osip Mandelstam compared his death to the death of Pushkin. The significance he attached to this event indicates that for Mandelstam, just as for Pasternak, the phenomenon of Skryabin transcended the composer's art.[12]

Skryabin's concept of art is an example of an extreme development of the romantic world view. Art, in Skryabin's view, possessed the power to transform the world and the life of mankind. The creative artist was for him a high priest through whose ministration this transformation would be achieved.[13]

Pasternak considered Skryabin's music composed around the turn of the century to be most influential on him. These years were a part of the acutely individualistic, Nietzschean

Nevertheless, the spiritual significance which the composer attached to his art is now all but meaningless" (*A History of Russian Music* [New York: The Macmillan Company, 1957], p. 211).

Insistence on ascribing extra-artistic significance to art, coupled with an inability to achieve a complete expression in art, was not unique with Skrjabin. This problem, not new to art, became especially acute within Russian symbolism. The cause of the problem is well elucidated by Vladislav Xodasevič. Xodasevič maintained that life and art were so unusually closely bound for the symbolists that their works became experiences and events of real life. According to Xodasevič, only a part of the creative energy of the symbolists was applied to their art; another part was used up in life. Symbolism for the symbolists was both an artistic method and a way of life. The fusion of the two prevented them from expressing themselves completely in their work (Vladislav Xodasevič, "O simvolizme," *Literaturnye stat'i i vospominanija* [New York: Chekhov Publishing House, 1954], pp. 156–57).

[12] Mandel'štam wrote in an unfinished article: "Puškin and Skrjabin are the two transformations of the same sun, the two transformations of the same heart. Twice the death of a creative artist brought the Russian people together and kindled a sun over them" (Osip Mandel'štam, "Puškin i Skrjabin," *Sobranie sočinenij v trex tomax* [Inter-Language Literary Associates, 1967–71], Vol. II, p. 313).

[13] Skrjabin's projected, but never realized, last work, *Mysterium*, was to unite music, poetry, and dance. The composer attached great significance to this work and had grandiose plans for its performance in India. Apparently, he believed that a performance of this work would actually lead to a transformation of mankind (B. F. Šlecer, *A. Skrjabin* [Berlin: Grani, 1923], Vol. I).

period in the composer's life. Skryabin's extreme individualism, his egocentrism and exceptionally high valuation of his own personality, were the elements that made a strong impact on Pasternak. To his thirteen-year-old admirer, Skryabin appeared as a deity fully aware of its own worth. It is significant that the dominant elements of Skryabin's influence on Pasternak—his individualism and faith in the creative powers of an individual—in the end proved to be the source of Pasternak's decision to break with music.

Both in *Safe Conduct* and in *Autobiographical Sketch* Pasternak tries to explain why he gave up music after six years of serious study and after an unequivocally high appraisal of his compositions by Skryabin himself. In *Safe Conduct*, Pasternak says that his decision was formed outside his consciousness. He maintains that his own reality differed from the objective reality; although he realized that the actual meaning of Skryabin's verdict was positive and, in fact, could not be disguised as anything else, at the same time he knew with absolute certainty that the objective meaning of Skryabin's evaluation had nothing to do with his own subjective reaction to it. As the source of doubt regarding his own possibilities as a musician, Pasternak names his lack of absolute pitch.

According to the version given in *Autobiographical Sketch*, however, it was a general discrepancy between his musical thought and its practical realization that Pasternak could not endure. By that time his theoretical studies were quite advanced, whereas the technical aspects were seriously lagging behind. Pasternak admits that, although he was seriously composing at the time, he could not read music with sufficient ease and could barely play the piano. In agreement with his mystical mood of that period, he interpreted his lack of absolute pitch as a sign from above that music was not his calling.

The origin of this fatal gap between inspiration and craftsmanship Pasternak traces back to Skryabin's influence. The egocentrism that permeated the composer's personality, according to Pasternak, was permissible in his case only;

when assumed by an adolescent it inevitably led to disastrous results. The imitation of Skryabin's egocentrism and the assigning of an absolute value to the powers of a creative artist produced in Pasternak a childishly arrogant attitude toward the noncreative aspects of work: "I despised everything uncreative, any kind of hack work, being conceited enough to imagine that I was a judge in these matters. In *real* life, I thought, everything must be a miracle, everything must be predestined from above, nothing must be deliberately designed or planned, nothing must be done to follow one's own fancies."[14]

Pasternak does not condemn Skryabin's individualism and egocentrism as such, because, in his opinion, it was the development that these ideas underwent in the young admirer of the master rather than the ideas themselves that were at fault. Pasternak does not dismiss Skryabin's Nietzscheanism, with its admixture of Russian maximalism, as an erroneous view; on the contrary, he maintains that in order to be meaningful and equal to its own potentialities, everything in this world should surpass itself. To attain a character of its own, all human activity has to contain a seed of infinity: "Actually, not only music must be super-music to mean anything, but everything in the world must surpass itself in order to be itself. Man, activity of man must include an element of infinity which lends shape and character to any phenomenon."[15]

It can be deduced from Pasternak's rather veiled statements that Skryabin's immediate influence on him was confined to a short period in his life. He indicates that the music Skryabin wrote after 1908 had no influence on him. In 1916, a year after the composer's death, he refers to the theory of synthesis of arts—to the implementation of which the last few years of Skryabin's life were devoted—as "ideas that reveal in a weary artist a previously concealed dilettante."[16] In *Doctor Zhivago*,

[14] *Sočinenija*, II, 11.

[15] *Ibid.*, II, 12.

[16] Pasternak's review of Majakovskij's *Prostoe, kak myčanie*. "Kritičeskie ètjudy," in *Literaturnaja Rossija*, March 19, 1965, pp. 18–19.

Vedenyapin complains that he had to listen to a reading of "a text in verse by the Symbolist A to the cosmogonic symphony by the composer B, with the spirits of the planets, voices of the four elements, etc., etc."[17] Vedenyapin's objections to the extremes of symbolism undoubtedly reflect Pasternak's own critical attitude. At the same time, certain elements of Skryabin's influence that can be identified with the romantic world view Pasternak retained throughout his long life. Among these are a faith in the individual and his almost unlimited potentialities and a firm belief in the transforming powers of art.

In 1909 Pasternak transferred from the law faculty of Moscow University to the philosophical section of the historico-philological faculty. The next three years of his life were to be devoted to the study of philosophy. At the university he found himself associating with the followers of the Marburg School of Neo-Kantianism and in 1912 he spent the summer term studying at the University of Marburg.

In commenting on the Marburg School, Pasternak limits his statements to a few remarks about the methods of the school and allows himself no discussion of its views. The school's selective and critical attitude toward the historical heritage and its break with routine were especially attractive to the young Pasternak. His concise remarks in *Safe Conduct* indicate that faithfulness to the critical method and interest in the "fact of science" convinced him of the independence and originality of Marburg Neo-Kantianism.

Toward the end of the summer term in Marburg Pasternak was entirely submerged in his work, but, he remarks, to an experienced observer his enthusiasm would have revealed a basically unscholarly attitude. Pasternak approached the subject too emotionally. He tended to digress instead of pursuing one idea to the end, and instead of searching for truth he attempted to confirm his intuitive notions.[18] The end of Pasternak's philosophical studies came sooner than could be expected.

[17] *Sočinenija*, IV, 43.   [18] *Ibid.*, II, 239.

The sisters V., the older of whom for several years had been the object of his affections, visited Pasternak in Marburg. This visit speeded up the decisive encounter: Pasternak proposed and was refused. This incident was a source both of bitterness and immeasurable misery, and at the same time of an unusually acute, complete, and new experience of existence, which brought about the birth of the poet in Pasternak. The period of search was over. Although Pasternak continued his formal studies upon his return to Moscow and in the spring of 1913 graduated from the university, after Marburg poetry became his only serious concern.

Pasternak's break with philosophy was as decisive as his break with music. His recently published letters from that period give the sequence of events, which closely resembles his reaction in 1909 when he decided to give up music. Pasternak speaks of his great respect and admiration for Hermann Cohen, whom he calls a "superman," and of Cohen's invitation to continue his studies at Marburg as a great honor, but the possibility of becoming a scholar, a German university professor, apparently was not only completely unexpected, but even somehow offensive to him. Pasternak concedes his inability to explain why he so "epileptically recoiled" from that path at the time when he had achieved his first notable success on it.[19] His farewell to philosophy and to his youth at the time of his departure from Marburg for Italy should be taken quite literally.[20] Pasternak knew that the period of search was over and that philosophy had joined music as a past stage of his development on the way to poetry.

THE BIRTH OF THE POET

After recovering from the shock of V.'s refusal, Pasternak noticed that surrounding objects were transformed: "Only

[19] "Čudo poètičeskogo voploščenija" (Pis'ma Borisa Pasternaka), *Voprosy Literatury*, No. 9, 1972. Letters of July 19 and 22, 1912 to A. L. Štix, pp. 142–43.
[20] *Ibid.*, II, 251.

now was I struck by what probably had begun earlier, but all
the time was overshadowed by the proximity of that which had
happened. . . . I was surrounded by transformed objects. Something not previously experienced had crept into the essence of
reality."[21] The unusual sharpening of the senses enabled the
poet to see a new world. A new dimension of life presented
itself to him: "Birds, houses and dogs, trees and horses, tulips
and people had become more concise and terse than childhood
had known them. A fresh laconicism of life was revealed to
me; it crossed the street, took me by the hand and led me
along the sidewalk."[22] The birth of a poet in Pasternak
coincided with his sudden maturity. He saw people and objects
in a new way, not the way he used to see them in his childhood.
Suddenly he realized that he was a part of the adult world and
on an equal footing with life's actuality.

This new vision of the world was not a transitory state.
Pasternak first became aware of it in Berlin, where he traveled
with the sisters V.; upon his return from this impromptu trip,
he could hardly recognize Marburg, so changed did the town
and its surroundings appear to him. In the poem "Marburg"
(1915, 1928) Pasternak speaks of his experience as a second
birth and develops the idea of beginning life anew. The age-old
instinct of self-preservation watches the poet as he is learning
to walk again:

'Научишься шагом, а после хоть в бег',
Твердил он, и новое солнце с зенита
Смотрело, как сызнова учат ходьбе
Туземца планеты на новой планиде.[23]

Once you learn to walk, you may run, if you wish,
Repeated he over and over, and a new sun in its zenith
Watched a native of the planet once again
Being taught to walk anew on his predestined world.

[21] *Ibid.*, II, 238.
[22] *Ibid.*
[23] *Ibid.*, I, 474. The original version in *Sočinenija*, I, 386–88, and the
final on pp. 220–22 of the same volume.

The interrelation of love and creativity is one of the essential intuitions of Pasternak's conception of art and, not unexpectedly, a recurrent theme in his work. In a short prose work "Letters from Tula" (1918) a young poet writes three letters to the woman whom he loves and from whom he has just parted. His first two letters speak of his love and the suffering caused by their parting. Like Pasternak at the time of his Marburg experience, the poet undergoes an unusual heightening of his perceptive powers. He suddenly discerns the difference between the true and false in art. In his third and last letter the theme of love and suffering is absent altogether.[24]

The same theme occupies a central position in *A Tale* (1929). As in other instances, passion serves as a catalyst to creativity; once the creative process is set in motion, creativity displaces passion from its foremost position. When the protagonist declares his love, he is overwhelmed by his own emotion and breaks down in sobs. This outburst of emotion inevitably leads to an outburst of creative passion. The function of love as a precursor of creativity is demonstrated almost graphically. The protagonist begins to write and becomes so engrossed in his work that he not only forgets about the object of his love, but actually does not notice her when she enters his room.[25]

For Pasternak, the intensity of emotions and the direct and spontaneous expression of them are essential elements of artistic creativity. The poet has to be in the thicket of impressions. In "Февраль. Достать чернил и плакать!" ("February. [It's time to] Get ink and weep," 1913) the news of the yet distant approach of spring affects the poet in a highly emotional way. He declares a desire to write about February, "bursting with sobs"—*навзрыд*. The word *навзрыд* reappears at the end of the poem, recapitulating the emotional quality of the whole process. Verse comes about spontaneously, unplanned and unpremeditated, under the influence of direct, immediate emotion:

[24] *Ibid.*, II, 75–80.
[25] *Ibid.*, II, 190.

> И чем случайней, тем вернее
> Слагаются стихи навзрыд.[26]

> And the more accidental, the better
> Are the verses composed bursting with sobs.

Intensity of emotion and spontaneity of response to life are shown as fundamental elements of the creative process in "Apelles' Mark" (1915), Pasternak's first published prose work. The title and the epigraph recall the story of the famous Greek painter Apelles, an artist who proved his identity through his art.

In Pasternak's story, a proof of his identity as an artist is demanded from a young poet who immediately responds to this challenge. The suggested topic for his reply is love. In a very short message to his challenger, the poet manages to convey what to him is a most striking characteristic of love: a new view of familiar things. The names of two lovers suddenly acquire for them an entirely new sound and meaning. But this is only the theoretical part of the poet's answer. He contrives to meet his challenger's lover and, in a most theatrical fashion, attempts to seduce her. Amidst his effusive and almost farcical declarations he suddenly notices how beautiful the woman before him is. Here ends the episode as a creation of the poet's imagination, and the real emotion takes over.[27]

The borderline between life and art is almost completely obliterated in the story. By exercising his creative imagination, the poet is creating life. The works of art as such are not Pasternak's concern here. It is the interrelationship of life and art, of passion and creativity, and the tangible imprint that artistic creativity leaves on life that he emphasizes.

---

[26] *Ibid.*, I, 177.

[27] The story has been interpreted as Pasternak's manifesto in opposition to symbolism. The young poet Heine, a realist, defeats Relinquimini, a symbolist, by responding to his challenge not with words but with deeds (Michel Aucouturier, "Il Tratto di Apelle. Manifeste littéraire du modernisme russe," *Revue des études slaves*, XLVII [1968], pp. 157–61).

In an early poem "Я рос. Меня, как Ганимеда" ("I grew.
I, like a Ganymede"), love is outdistanced by poetic inspiration, but both exist side by side in the same world:

Дни далеко, когда предтечей,
Любовь, ты надо мной плыла.

Но разве мы не в том же небе?
На то и прелесть высоты,
Что, как себя отпевший лебедь,
С орлом плечо к плечу и ты.[28]

Those days are far away, when as a forerunner
You, love, sailed above me.

But are we not in the same sky?
This is the enchantment of elevation—
That you—as a swan who has sung its song—
Are shoulder to shoulder with the eagle.

Pasternak interprets passion more broadly than in its usual
meaning. In *Safe Conduct* he explains that it stands for the
concept of energy and of man's potentialities. In his notes on
translating Shakespeare (published in 1956) he speaks of
passion not as a condition of one's soul but as a fundamental
principle of the world. It is a cosmic element that only pretends
to be subdued. In a poem in *Сестра моя жизнь* (*My Sister,
Life*) the whole world is seen as the result of "the discharges
of passion":

И сады, и пруды, и ограды,
И кипящее белыми воплями
Мирозданье—лишь страсти разряды,
Человеческим сердцем накопленной.

The gardens, and the ponds, and the fences,
And the cosmos boiling with white howls
Are only the discharges of passion
Stored up by human heart.

[28] *Sočinenija*, I, 180.

Artistic creativity results from the accumulation of emotional energy. Once it is brought to life, it overshadows other phenomena, including love itself:

Накрывает ладонью, как шашки,
Сон и совесть, и ночь, и любовь оно.[29]

It covers with its hand, as [it would] checkers,
Sleep and conscience, night and love.

Passion is what art attempts to depict; it is the subject of art. The figurative language of art, according to Pasternak, is the direct language of passion. The highest achievement that art can hope to attain is to overhear the true voice of love.[30]

One of the aspects of the poet's new vision of life was the knowledge that it was not a one-sided experience; Pasternak was confident that surrounding life suddenly recognized him too and that this recognition was of a permanent nature. He seemed to realize that he was being chosen by life and that by accepting this proposed brotherhood with life he was concluding a lifelong pact: "Less than ever was I deserving of brotherhood with this enormous summer sky. But at the moment this was not mentioned. For the time being I was forgiven everything. Some time in the future I was to pay for the morning's trust. And everything around me was vertiginously reliable, like a law, according to which *such* loans are always repaid."[31]

Pasternak stresses the difference between his previous involvement in philosophy and his new and total submersion in poetry. Although he was oblivious to his surroundings and to life outside his room both before and after his trip to Berlin, he sensed a marked difference in his relationship to the outside world after his "second birth." Before, he was isolated from

[29] *Ibid.*, I, 24.
[30] *Ibid.*, III, 198. Apparently Pasternak's article "Zametki k perevodam šekspirovskix tragedij" was written sometime in the early forties (see *Sočinenija*, III, 261).
[31] *Ibid.*, II, 238.

the world; now he was joining in with the life around him. The new poetic vision of the world brought with it a communing with life and nature that proved to be one of the most lasting experiences of the poet Pasternak.

Although Pasternak started writing poetry before his Marburg summer, until then he did not consider it a serious involvement. As he wrote in *Safe Conduct*, at that time he saw his versifying experiments as an "unfortunate weakness" and as a sign of immaturity that he carefully concealed from his friends. In Marburg he started writing regularly and seriously. Most of the poems of Pasternak's first book of verse were written during the following summer (1913). At that time, the writing of poetry became his constant occupation, a necessity, and a source of inimitable joy: "For the first time in my life I wrote poetry not as a rare exception, but often and continuously, as one paints or composes music. I felt a strong need to write those verses, to scratch out and to restore what had been scratched out. It brought an incomparable pleasure to me that moved me to tears."[32]

THE POET AND THE WORLD

The realization that the life around him takes part in the poet's emotions and experiences is a fundamental element of Pasternak's poetic conception and is present in his work beginning with the earliest poems. In "Сегодня мы исполним грусть его" ("Today we shall act his melancholy," 1913), the whole city participates in the poet's dejection. He endows his surroundings with his own emotion. The poet's feeling is central; the concrete objects of the world around him illustrate his condition; and in the background, as in the poem "Marburg," there is life ("В тылу шла жизнь"), of whose permanent collaboration the poet is assured. In an earlier version of this poem the closing lines point more explicitly to an active participation of the surroundings:

[32] *Ibid.*, II, 31, 32.

О, город мой, весь день, весь день сегодня
Не сходит с уст твоих печаль моя![33]

O my city, all day, all day today
My sadness never leaves your lips.

The experience of nature's and life's participation in his emotions leads the poet to a feeling of equality and brotherhood with the whole universe. He becomes a part of the miraculous night where the far and the near fuse:

Со мной, с моей свечою вровень
Миры расцветшие висят.

With me, on the level with my candle
The blossoming worlds are suspended.

He dissolves in this night, "converts" to it:

И, как в неслыханную веру,
Я в эту ночь перехожу.[34]

And I join this night,
As I would an unheard-of faith.

The poet becomes a part of the garden at night, which assumes the dimensions of the universe.

In *Safe Conduct*, trying to elucidate the interrelationship of man and nature, Pasternak maintains that nature is introduced into poetry so as to depict the poet's passion, and, conversely, human passion is depicted so as to bring in nature: the two elements appear to be equal and completely interchangeable. A description of a wholesale flower market in the same section of *Safe Conduct* is a good example of man and nature sharing emotions and representing each other. The poet is especially tempted to visit the market in the early spring. The luminous March twilight frequenting the filthy rooms of a cheap hotel and restraining the poet at the door, the suddenly appearing and whispering street, the staccato steps of the

---

[33] *Ibid.*, I, 378.
[34] *Ibid.*, I, 177–78.

spring air, and the shivering outlines of the street are introduced in order to convey the poet's sudden awareness of the
approaching spring.

Flowers stand for the essence of seasonal change, the
wisdom of ever-returning life. The poet feels a part of this
cosmic rejuvenation, but the emotions that this realization
calls forth in him are attributed to the flowers. The excitement
of the poet is carried over to them; they rage, breathe, become
agitated: "In enormous tubs, sheaves of peonies, yellow
daisies, tulips, and anemones, sorted out according to colors
and varieties, raged in competition with the lamps. They
breathed and were agitated, as if grappling with each other."[35]

Despite this apparent equality of man and nature in Pasternak's poetic scheme, it is, undoubtedly, man who occupies
the central position: his individuality is never dissolved in his
surroundings. Nature actually lives man's emotions. When a
bog is feverish, a forest depressed, a meadow nauseated, a
room trembling, or a city—dusty and exhausted from travel—
is falling into bed, there is little doubt that those sensations,
responses, and actions are the poet's.[36] Nature's sharing man's
emotions emphasizes his predominance. This anthropocentric
attitude is especially noticeable in *Doctor Zhivago*. After
Lara's departure from Varykino, Zhivago vividly experiences
nature's participation in his grief. According to Lara, the
whole world wanted them to love each other.[37] The idea of
the collaboration of man and nature is of primary concern for
Zhivago himself. He expresses his thoughts on the subject by
attempting to formulate his theory of mimicry. He sees the
adaptation to one's surroundings, an aspect of the process of
natural selection, as the result of the effort of an individual
will. For Zhivago, even color adaptation in insects is a tangible
expression of the will of an individual.[38]

Life's and nature's concern for the poet is the subjective
aspect of Pasternak's new poetic vision that allows him to experience the mutual interdependence of things and phenomena

[35] *Ibid.*, II, 218–19.   [36] *Ibid.*, I, 90, 89, 38, 42.
[37] *Ibid.*, IV, 463, 513.   [38] *Ibid.*, IV, 356, 418.

on a broader scope. Visually it manifests itself as the unusual sharpness of individual details:

Я вышел на площадь. Я мог быть сочтен
Вторично родившимся. Каждая малость
Жила и, не ставя меня ни во что,
В прощальном значеньи своем подымалась.

I walked out onto the square. I could be regarded
As someone born for the second time. Every detail
Lived and, disregarding me entirely,
Arose in its departing significance.

The details gain in importance because they do not stand by themselves but are signs of the whole. The poet is able to perceive the distant past by a few details that link it to the present. Marburg's historical past looks at him from the trees and the houses:

Тут жил Мартин Лютер. Там—братья Гримм.
Когтистые крыши. Деревья. Надгробья.
И все это помнит и тянется к ним.
Все—живо. И все это тоже—подобья.[39]

Here lived Martin Luther. Over there—the brothers Grimm.
Sharp-clawed roofs. Trees. Gravestones.
And all this remembers them and reaches out to them.
All is alive. And all is analogies.

In *Safe Conduct*, describing the transformation of the surrounding world by poetic vision, Pasternak stresses that this new vision enables the poet to perceive the whole by means of an individual detail. In his new world, a part stands for the whole. This premise, it seems, is the source of the complexity and often-mentioned incomprehensibility of Pasternak's early verse and prose. One element represents the whole, and if the reader's attention remains affixed to this element, the whole evades him. What he sees are distortion of distances and outlines and the dismemberment of objects.

---

[39] *Ibid.*, I, 220–21.

The reader has to exercise creative association in order to follow the poet: to be aware of the boundaries removed between objects, to reconstruct the whole by one detail. Pasternak practically foretells the judgment of his poetry as difficult and incomprehensible when in "Вассерманова реакция" ("Wassermann Test")—an article written in 1914— he says that, traditionally, the reading public considers "association by similarity," which he rejects for its facility, as an essential characteristic of poetry in general.

The poetic trope that Pasternak employs to convey the interrelation of things is metonymy. In "Wassermann Test," attempting a description of what in his opinion is basic to the "metaphorical vision of the world," Pasternak, without naming it, describes metonymy and explains his predilection for metonymic expression. This trope, according to him, is comparable to an intricate lock, the key to which is in the poet's possession. The reader can only peek through the keyhole at that which is concealed within. A poet who resorts to similarity as the basis for constructing his tropes tosses the keys into the hands of "the amateurs from the crowd." Contiguity rather than similarity should, in Pasternak's opinion, be at the basis of metaphorical association, for it is contiguity that possesses the quality of necessity and the dramatic quality mandatory for metaphorical expression. For him it is the "morbid necessity" of bringing together dissimilar but proximate objects that gives life to an image: "The word,—impenetrable in its coloring,—cannot adopt the coloring of the object compared. . . . A notion can be colored only through the morbid necessity of bringing together, of that 'strip-farming' [intermittence] which reigns in lyrically compressed consciousness." [40]

[40] "Vassermanova reakcija," *Rukonog*, Sbornik stixov i kritiki (Moskva: Centrifuga, 1914), p. 37. The importance of metonymy in Pasternak's work was pointed out by Roman Jakobson, who saw Pasternak's originality in the utilization of the metonymic rather than metaphoric series both in his verse and prose. Jakobson's article, "Randbemerkungen zur Prosa des Dichters Pasternak," *Slavische Rundschau*, No. 6 (1935), pp. 357–74, analyzes metonymy in Pasternak's prose.

If at the basis of metaphor is comparison or opposition, metonymy depends on proximity of objects taken in a very broad sense. This general "proximity" includes causal relationships, various relationships of a part to the whole, physical proximity of otherwise unrelated objects (proximity in the narrow sense), temporal relationship of events, etc. Consequently, one characteristic detail can stand for an object as a whole, an effect can represent the cause, an expression of emotion can signify the subject who is experiencing it, physical surroundings can be endowed with the emotions and perceptions of the lyrical hero, two events can be united by their concurrence in time. This "metonymic vision of the world" is largely responsible for the originality of Pasternak's verse. But whether it is metonymy or metaphor in a narrow sense, at the basis of the association of the two objects almost invariably is proximity.

In "Плачущий сад"[41] ("The Weeping Garden," *My Sister, Life*), the process by which nature assumes the emotions and the responses of the lyrical hero is given in slow motion. The poet watches the garden through a window of his room. It is raining. The two proximate objects in this case are the poet and the garden. In stanza one the garden (a masculine gender noun in Russian) is dripping with rain and listening:

Ужасный!—Капнет и вслушается:
Всё он ли один на свете
Мнет ветку в окне, как кружевце,
Или есть свидетель.

It is terrible! It drips and listens:
Is it still alone in the world—
Crumpling a branch like lace in the window—
Or is there a witness.

In stanza four the poet listens to the sounds around him:

[41] *Sočinenija*, I, 6–7.

26

К губам поднесу и прислушаюсь:
Всё я ли один на свете,—
Готовый навзрыд при случае,—
Или есть свидетель.

I lift it to my lips and listen:
Am I still alone in the world—
Ready to burst out in sobs if need be—
Or is there a witness.

The almost complete identity of lines two and four, and of the verbs *вслушается* and *прислушаюсь* of line one in both stanzas, not only suggests a parallel between a weeping person inside and the dripping garden outside, but superimposes the two and makes them fuse.

Being convinced that there is no one around, the garden continues its dripping (stanza three):

Ни звука. И нет соглядатаев.
В пустынности удостоверясь,
Берется за старое—скатывается
По кровле, за желоб и через.

Not a sound. No spies.
Convinced that there is no one around,
It lapses into its old ways—rolls down
The roof, past the drainpipe and beyond.

In the last stanza the actions of the poet parallel the actions of the garden:

Но тишь. И листок не шелохнется.
Ни признака зги, кроме жутких
Глотков и плескания в шлепанцах,
И вздохов, и слез в промежутке.

But it's silence. Not even a leaf stirs.
Not a sign of light, only frightful
Gulps and sloshing of slippers,
And sighs, and tears in between.

Но тишь of the poet stanza corresponds to *ни звука* of the garden stanza. The rest of the line indicates that the poet is alone, but the surroundings of the poet and the garden are made to exchange places. The poet's solitude is described in terms of the immobility of the garden, "*И листок не шелохнется,*" whereas the garden is satisfied that there are no witnesses to its actions, "*И нет соглядатаев.*" Through this exchange of the surroundings, a more complete identification of the poet and the garden is achieved.

Thus a cliché metaphor "rain drops—tear drops" appears in a completely new guise. The title suggests that the garden is a human being; the masculine gender of the Russian *сад* enhances this suggestion. But only in stanza four, while identifying the lyrical hero with the weeping garden, does the poet introduce the word *навзрыд*, which points to human sobbing. Tears are mentioned, but in the very last line of the poem.

In "Заместительница"[42] ("A Substitute," *My Sister, Life*), a photograph acts like the person depicted. The picture, a substitute for the living woman who is away, comes to life:

Я живу с твоей карточкой, с той, что хохочет,
У которой суставы в запястьях хрустят,
Той, что пальцы ломает и бросить не хочет,
У которой гостят и гостят и грустят.

I live with your photograph, with the one that is laughing,
Whose wrists are crackling,
That which is wringing her hands and wouldn't let go,
At whose side one stays for a long time, dejected.

The beginning of the first line is addressed to the subject of the picture, the end defines the picture as the laughing one. In the next line, although the grammar suggests that this is a continuation of the description of the photograph, her wrists are crackling and, obviously, the real woman takes over. The opening of line four, suggests the woman at whose place one's

---

[42] *Ibid.*, I, 26.

visits tend to be prolonged, but the last word of the line returns to the poet's dejected mood brought on by her absence: he is not visiting at her house, but lingers over her picture for a long time. This ambiguity helps to achieve a more complete fusion of the real woman with her picture (the Russian word for picture is of feminine gender).

In the next three stanzas the picture-woman is moving around the house, waltzing, adjusting her hair, attaching a flower to her dress. In the last stanza she is hurriedly "swallowing the refreshing sections of a tangerine" and crumpling its peelings in her hand. The description of the picture blends with the description of the woman herself; her visual image brings to the poet's mind—and to the poem—the living woman: her manners, her actions, and even her destiny:

Провальсировать к славе, шутя, полушалок
Закусивши, как муку, и еле дыша.

Jokingly, to waltz to glory,
Biting the shawl like one's lips in pain, and being
     out of breath.

In a poem of the cycle "Болезнь" ("Illness," *Themes and Variations*), a man's course of illness is superimposed upon the concurrent changes in the weather. The snowstorm repeats the febrile fluctuations of the sick man's temperature:

Больной следит. Шесть дней подряд
Смерчи беснуются без устали.
По кровле катятся, бодрят,
Бушуют, падают в бесчувствии.[43]

The sick man is watching. For six days in a row
Storms have been raging incessantly.
They roll along the roof, they are invigorating,
They rampage, they fall in a swoon.

This record of meteorological observations actually very precisely describes the sensations and the reactions of a human

[43] *Ibid.,* I, 70.

body to a fever: agitation stimulated by the rising temperature and the overwhelming weakness resulting from the abrupt fall of temperature.

The man is delirious in stanza two: Christmas and New Year's Eve are lost in the storms, which do not subside. In the last stanza the illness takes a natural turn toward a recovery: the man falls asleep. This is reflected in the weather; the blizzard, which by now has assumed grandiose proportions, has some elements of calm in it: "Пурга, как океан / В величьи,—тихой называется" ("In its grandeur, the blizzard, like the ocean, is called 'pacific'"). The allusion to the Pacific Ocean points to the appearance of tranquility that the raging elements present at this moment.

In another poem of the same cycle, the nightshirt of a sick man leads an existence independent from its owner. First, it is asking for more heat and light: "То каплю тепла ей, то лампу придвинь" ("Now it needs more heat, now it wants the lamp moved closer"); then it recalls a skiing trip: "Ей помнятся лыжи."[44] The reminiscences about the skiing trip that follow are given from the point of view of the shirt. The personal pronoun "her," referring to the feminine gender nouns (фуфайка, кофта, фланель) used for the shirt, enhances the impression that it is a living being in its own right. In this case it is the actual physical proximity that endows the garment with the sensations and thoughts of the man wearing it.

In a poem about Petersburg and Peter the Great (1917), the creation becomes interchangeable with its creator. First, the parallel between the man and his creation, the city, is established by means of comparisons: "Тучи, как волосы, встали дыбом" and "Улицы рвутся, как мысли, к гавани" ("Clouds, like hair, are standing on end" and "Streets, like thoughts, rush toward the harbor"). Then the restlessness of Peter is identified with the inundating waters of the Neva, and in the last two lines the identification is completed when the sound of the upsurging waters is discovered to be Peter's

[44] *Ibid.*, I, 73.

delirious talk: "Это ведь бредишь ты, невменяемый, / Быстро бормочешь вслух" ("But it is you, unconscious and delirious, rapidly muttering out loud").[45]

Those critics who commented on Pasternak's use of the personification of nature usually sensed some differences in his practice from the traditional use of this device and were reluctant to refer to it as pathetic fallacy.[46] This point is discussed in great detail by Andrey Sinyavsky in his introduction to the 1965 edition of Pasternak's poetry.[47] The clue to the differences in Pasternak's practice from the conventional attribution of human characteristics to inanimate objects is provided, as Sinyavsky correctly observes, by Pasternak himself. In *A Tale*, when the protagonist perceives the city morning as the woman whom he loves, he is aware that this identification has been experienced before and points out what is new about his perception: his identification of a person with the surrounding objects is broader and more precise (*чувство было ... шире и точнее*).[48] Pasternak's is a very subtle and extremely varied use of personification. The difference is in the degree to which it is carried. It is not limited to nature, for practically any object in the poet's surroundings can be used to depict man. On the other hand, Pasternak's personification is not vague or general, but very specific. What is most striking about his use of this device, however, is the complete elimination of comparison and a sustained development of the correspondence. Pasternak does not suggest that Serezha sees the city morning as Anna, but makes him realize how "painful and difficult" it is for her *to be* the city morning. He watches how she "slowly throws back her brick Gothic towers."

[45] *Ibid.*, I, 195.

[46] See, for instance, Isaiah Berlin, "The Energy of Pasternak," *Partisan Review*, 1950, pp. 748–51; and Helen Muchnic, *op.cit.*, pp. 381–82.

[47] A. Sinjavskij, "Poèzija Pasternaka," an introductory article in Boris Pasternak, *Stixotvorenija i poèmy* (Biblioteka poèta, Bol'šaja serija; Moskva-Leningrad: Sovetskij Pisatel', 1965), pp. 9–62 (this edition is later referred to as *Stixotvorenija*).

[48] *Sočinenija*, II, 196.

Pasternak's personification is a mutual interaction rather than a one-way movement: nature is depicted by means of human characteristics, and man is defined through nature. There is a close correspondence between the two; one is a continuation of the other. At the basis of this is Pasternak's experience of cosmic unity, which, however, does not destroy man's personal identity. Man does not disappear in nature, nor is nature there only as a representation of man's emotions; both are a part of a whole, closely and intimately related. Therefore a mutual response between the two is not something unexpected.

In *Safe Conduct*, Pasternak described his impressions of Venice in terms of the sound of a guitar. Hearing the sound, he looked out of the window: he looked for the sound. This synesthetic response illustrates his perception of the whole by one detail. For Pasternak, the sound of the guitar came to represent Venice, to stand for Venice as a whole. Elsewhere in *Safe Conduct* he insists that the details of the poet's surroundings are not arranged in a hierarchical order. Each and every one of them is capable of representing the essence of the phenomenon of which it is a part, because his intuition enables the artist to perceive beyond the façade of vivid details the essence and the meaning of things.

For the adolescent heroine of "Детство Люверс" ("Childhood of Luvers"), however, who is not a poet and who only by virtue of her age has a more direct perception of things, the two do not go together. The visual vividness of the picture exists by itself without any meaning. When meaning is brought into the picture, its visual attraction decreases, it loses in color and brightness. The graphic quality of the long-familiar picture of the drilling of the soldiers is destroyed the very moment it acquires human significance.[49] The disjointed aspects, the outward vividness and the inner meaning, are integrated by poetic intuition.

Aided by his poetic intuition, the poet perceives life not as a multitude of disconnected details, but as a meaningful

[49] *Ibid.*, II, 111.

whole. Thus a picture of the moving vehicles makes the poet instantly aware of human aspirations that are at the source of this activity: "Carts, bicycles, trucks, and trains began to move in all directions. Above them, like invisible plumes wreathed human plans and desires. They steamed and moved with the conciseness of familiar parables, which are comprehensible without explanations."[50] Intuition, an ability to grasp the whole (*цельное познание*), to get at once at the essence of things, is the quality with which Pasternak endows his Doctor Zhivago; it characterizes him both as a poet and a doctor.[51]

As early as 1914 Pasternak wrote that a poet (*лирический деятель*) stands above all for an integrating principle. Compared to the process of integration, the parts that are being integrated are relatively insignificant. The element that justifies the existence of a poem, Pasternak terms "lyrical integral" or "theme." He defines it only negatively, saying that it is neither the central idea nor the literary plot.[52] It is a dynamic principle diametrically opposed to anything constant and static, the "integrating principle" that evades definition.

THE DYNAMISM OF ART

Even a casual reader of Pasternak's poetry cannot fail to observe the predominance of raging elements over stable conditions in his nature and a virtual lack of static scenes and immovable objects in his poetry in general. In nature's inexhaustible source of dynamism lies one of its chief attractions for Pasternak:

Природа ж—ненадежный элемент.
Ее вовек оседло не поселишь.
Она всем телом алчет перемен,
И вся цветет из дружной жажды зрелищ.[53]

[50] *Ibid.*, II, 238.
[51] *Ibid.*, IV, 106–07, 418.
[52] "Vassermanova reakcija," *op.cit.*, pp. 35–36.
[53] *Sočinenija*, I, 292.

But nature is not dependable.
It cannot be forced to stay put.
It thirsts for change with its whole body.
And it blooms due to a concerted desire for something
   spectacular.

He is naturally attracted to storms and is afraid of calm:

Мне страшен штиль. И мне страшна,
Как близкий взвизг летучей мыши,
Таких затиший тишина,
Такая тишина затиший.[54]

I fear calm seas. I fear—
As [I fear] the nearby screech of a bat—
The silence of such calm,
The calm of such silences.

There is an abundance of thunderstorms and snowstorms in
his poetry; if not the storm itself, it is usually its approach
or its aftereffects that he chooses to talk about. In "Июльская
гроза" ("A Storm in July," 1917), the thunderstorm is running
up the stairs:

Гроза в воротах! на дворе!
Преображаясь и дурея,
Во тьме, в раскатах, в серебре,
Она бежит по галерее.

По лестнице. И на крыльцо.
Ступень, ступень, ступень.—Повязку!
У всех пяти зеркал лицо
Грозы, с себя сорвавшей маску.[55]

A thunderstorm is at the gates! in the yard!
Transforming itself and dazed,
In the dark, in a roar of thunder, in silver flashes
It dashes along the veranda.

[54] *Stixotvorenija*, p. 627.
[55] *Sočinenija*, I, 208.

Up the stairs. And to the porch.
A step, a step, a step—take off the blindfold!
All five mirrors have the face
Of thunderstorm with its mask torn off.

In "Приближение грозы" ("The Approach of a Storm," 1927), although acting more calmly, the storm is moving in and taking over:

Ты близко. Ты идешь пешком
Из города—и тем же шагом
Займешь обрыв, взмахнешь мешком
И гром прокатишь по оврагам.[56]

You are nearby. You walk on foot
From the city—and at the same pace
You will occupy the precipice, wave your knapsack,
And roll the thunder through the ravines.

In "Июль" ("July," 1956), the summer month becomes the poet's summer tenant, who is described in terms of his activity:

Везде болтается некстати,
Мешается во все дела,
В халате крадется к кровати,
Срывает скатерть со стола.

Ног у порога не обтерши,
Вбегает в вихре сквозняка
И с занавеской, как с танцоршей,
Взвивается до потолка.[57]

Inopportune, he hangs about everywhere,
Interferes with everything,
Wearing a bathrobe, stealthily tiptoes to the bed,
Pulls the cloth from the table.

[56] *Ibid.*, I, 238.
[57] *Ibid.*, III, 68.

Not wiping his feet at the door,
Enters at a run in the whirlwind of a draft,
And, as if with a dancing partner,
Flies up to the ceiling with the curtain.

In the late twenties and the thirties, Pasternak's serious
Soviet critics had a hard time reconciling the acknowledged
prevalence of action over description in his poetry with the
confinement of the action to the immediate surroundings of
the lyrical hero. It was often argued that by depicting nature
through human emotions, movements, and actions, Pasternak
reduced even natural phenomena to the level of his *быт*, of
his everyday life and physical ambience and by this manifested
his unmistakably "bourgeois" colors.[58] Marina Tsvetaeva, a
reader both attentive and well attuned to Pasternak's poetry,
very aptly described his predilection for movement and action
as the dynamism of a man sitting at his desk.[59]

In *Safe Conduct*, speaking of the aims of art, Pasternak
contrasts it with science, which—using the empirical means at
its disposal—perceives natural phenomena visually, "in a
section of a column of light," in other words, is able to record
only a state. But since life is a dynamic process rather than a
state, a simple scientific statement of fact cannot keep up
with life's movement. While science is uttering its truth, life
marches on and scientific truth falls behind and becomes
deceptive.

The extraordinary means needed to keep up with life's
pace are provided by art, which concerns itself with the
presence of energy in life, with the dynamics of life; it depicts
life "traversed by a ray of energy." Art succeeds in not falling
behind the present by being ahead of it, by looking into the

[58] D. Oblomievskij, "Boris Pasternak," *Literaturnyj Sovremennik*, 4
(1934), pp. 127–42. A. Ležnev, "Boris Pasternak," *Sovremenniki* (Moscow,
1927), pp. 32–54.
[59] Marina Cvetaeva, "Èpos i lirika sovremennoj Rossii—Vladimir
Majakovskij i Boris Pasternak," *Novyj Grad* (Paris), No. 7 (1933), p. 73.
The first part of this article appeared in No. 6, pp. 28–41.

future. Likewise, by not being preoccupied with man's actual individual achievements and by speaking of his potentialities, it is capable of revealing the truth about man. As Pasternak puts it, in art a man's individual voice is silenced, and the image of man takes over.

Energy is the only "aspect of consciousness" that needs some tangible proof of its existence, because it is evident only at the moment of its appearance. Art is the only means capable of depicting energy: "Lasting only for the instant of its manifestation, energy can be expressed only by the shifting language of images, that is, by the language of the accompanying signs."[60] In terms of individual consciousness, energy is emotion. Human spirit cannot be confined to the material world; it transcends it. As Pasternak wrote in an early (1917) fragment: "... духу человека негде жить, / Когда не в мире, созданном вторично" ("Man's spirit has no place to live, if not in the world created anew").[61]

The material world, inert and static, calls for an active, creative interference, and this is art's sphere of action. Art attempts to achieve a transformation from a static to a dynamic state, to succeed in setting off the inert and the static at the speed matching life's, to induce the past to catch up with life's movement. The aim of art for Pasternak is in switching that which is being depicted "from the cold axles to the hot."

When Pasternak writes that his experience of the city did not correspond to the place where he lived, he is opposing the life in the realm of the spirit to the material world, the vivid exterior of which is a complete expression of its essence. Pasternak describes himself at the time when he was turning from music to poetry as being physically affected by this heavy world, which is untouched by the transforming spirit. These "attacks of chronic impatience" were his response to the all-pervasive rule of necessity. Human activity that implied an active application of an individual's will and energy to the

[60] *Sočinenija*, ii, 243–44. The preceding discussion is based on the passages found on pp. 234–35 and 242–44.

[61] *Stixotvorenija*, p. 529.

fabric of life did not cause this sensation in the young poet.[62] By investing his surroundings with his emotion, the poet endows the spiritually static material world with the dynamics of his own spiritual condition. Pasternak's dynamism is a dynamism of spirit. Physical storms and violent movement in his poetry are there to speak of this spiritual quality of life, the depiction of which is the poet's aim. Remaining within the limits of the familiar and the everyday, the poet is able to demonstrate the accessibility of the spiritual experience to man under normal conditions, to show that it does not require anything extraordinary.

From a certain point of view, however, Pasternak's implicit acceptance of *быт* appears contradictory. Apparently, for the young Pasternak comfort and affluence were very much a part of the material world of inertia; they not only threatened but actually were able to destroy the dynamism of life in an individual.[63] In *Safe Conduct* Pasternak wrote that in his youth he was haunted by a fear of more or less ordered and comfortable everyday life. Speaking of his trip to Marburg in the summer of 1912, he refers to his program of life abroad as "Spartan" and explains that the reason for this was not so much a matter of limited funds as of principle, which banished all comfort from his life. His tolerance for material comfort Pasternak connects with the post-revolutionary times and associates it with a radical break with his prewar existence. It is significant, however, that he speaks of that change as temporary.[64] The introduction to *Spektorsky* (1930) is one place where the poet obviously has a very negative view of the realia of his everyday life. This mood—of nostalgia for his childhood and of disappointment in his current surroundings ("Pots and razors, brushes, hair curlers")[65]—is so much unlike Pasternak's usual joyous acceptance of existence that it should be considered exceptional. Pasternak's attention to the details

[62] *Sočinenija*, II, 215–17.
[63] *Ibid.*, I, 87.
[64] *Ibid.*, II, 222.
[65] *Ibid.*, I, 278.

of everyday life increased with the passing years, to disconcert some of his critics, who saw in this attitude something unworthy of a great poet. For Yury Zhivago, the physical surroundings of one's life are imbued with the human emotions and aspirations that take place there and in this way are redeemed from their pettiness.

Pasternak retained his faith in the transforming powers of art until the very end. In 1958 he wrote of art as more powerful in changing life than the storms changing the face of nature:

Рука художника еще всесильней
Со всех вещей смывает грязь и пыль.
Преображенней из его красильни
Выходят жизнь, действительность и быль.[66]

The hand of an artist is even more omnipotent
In washing off dirt and dust from everything.
Life and reality appear more transformed
Coming out of the artist's dye-works.

His poet in *A Tale* (1929) described the immense power at the disposal of a creative artist in more paradoxical terms as capable of destroying both material objects and social institutions and conventions: "The power of this miracle is such, that without any effort it could crack the pelvis of a piano, demolishing at the same time the bones of the merchant class and 'Vienna chairs.'"[67] Art transforms everything it touches; it is not surprising, therefore, that in art both time and space are transcended. The poet attempts to "fit" a whole world onto a page: "Целый мир уложить на странице, / Уместиться в границах строфы. ("To confine a whole world to a page, to fit into the limits of a stanza," 1958).[68] Pushkin's poem "The Prophet" inspires Pasternak with a meditation on the subject of transcending space in art (*Themes and Variations*, 1923). Like Pushkin's prophet, who suddenly becomes aware of the

[66] *Ibid.*, ɪɪɪ, 105.
[67] *Ibid.*, ɪɪ, 191.
[68] *Ibid.*, ɪɪɪ, 92.

angelic orders as well as of the life of the animal and vegetable kingdoms, the poet perceives diverse geographical regions that come together in one point of space, the room where Pushkin's poem is being written: the desert where the prophet had his mystical experience, a port on the White Sea, Arkhangelsk, and the river Ganges.[69]

Time, like everything else in life, calls for man's creative interference. The poet realizes that time passes because we neglect it:

Вы поняли, что время бы не шло,
Когда б оно на нас не обижалось.[70]

You realized that time would not pass,
Had it not been offended by us.

In a prose fragment, published in 1937, the narrator repeatedly experiences a feeling of sadness upon arising from sleep at sundown: "The day, which had passed without my knowledge, was gone. ... With unquenchable sadness I looked at the crimson eye of the sunset, as at an attendant's lamp at the tail end of a train which had just pulled out from a station."[71] What offsets the meaningless passage of time is man's activity.

In art, however, the category of time assumes an entirely new dimension. Compared to human time, "time in art" is a transformed entity. Pasternak explains the essence of this transformation on the example of his translating of Swinburne's "Chastelard." A point in the life of the translator is superimposed upon a point in the life of the poet Swinburne and further upon a point in the life of the historical Mary Stuart, the heroine of the play. The time when the poet relives the life of the protagonist and the actual time of the protagonist's life (a historical character in this case) are projected into art, where the two different points in time become identical, "a real October

[69] *Ibid.*, i, 67.
[70] *Ibid.*, i, 288.
[71] *Ibid.*, ii, 318.

in art." In art, a poet lives the life of his hero, whether historical or fictional, and thus transcends time ("Несколько положений"[72] ["A Few Principles," 1922]).

The constant attempts of art to capture the temporary in life and to transform it into the eternal are realized through the personality of an artist. An artist's life becomes an instrument for comprehending life in general. This is what Pasternak meant when he wrote in "Черный бокал" ("Black Goblet," 1916) that the subjectivity of a lyrical poet is not just the subjectivity of an individual but the expression of the integral principle of originality immanent in lyrical poetry as such. "The original in an ideal sense," Pasternak suggests, should replace the ambiguous "subjectivity." *Лирика* (Lyrical Poetry) assumes a far more significant role than is usually assigned to it; it becomes an instrument eternity uses in its encroachments upon reality.[73]

In his notes on translating Shakespeare (published in 1956),[74] Pasternak speaks of the language of art, whether verbal or pictorial, as the only effectual means available to man for bridging the gap between the immensity of his goals and the shortness of his life. Metaphoric speech, "the shorthand of a great spirit," is the inevitable result of the artist's desire to include the whole world in his work; as such it serves as a weapon in man's struggle against passing time.

[72] *Ibid.*, III, 153–54.
[73] *Ibid.*, III, 149–50.
[74] *Ibid.*, III, 194.

CHAPTER TWO

Art and Reality

"Она жила, как *alter ego*,
И я назвал ее сестрой."
(*Сочинения*, III, 139)

"*She lived as my* alter ego,
And I called her my sister."

PASTERNAK possessed an unusual synthesizing capacity that often enabled him to achieve in his work a successful integration of various divergent elements. The essential unity of the cosmos was a real and all-pervasive experience for the poet. It manifested itself through the interdependence and virtual equality in his work between the poet and nature or the surrounding world in general.

Pasternak's propensity to integrate is evident in his conscious attempt to keep the phonetics of the word in balance with its meaning and in his insistence on an inherent unity between form and content in a work of art. What underlies these integrating tendencies is Pasternak's unambiguous assertion of a close interrelation of art and reality; this is one of the basic and consistent tenets of his aesthetics. It is also the premise from which stems Pasternak's interpretation of the term "realism." His reiteration of the apparently self-evident truth that a work of art has as its starting point the experience of reality suggests that the realization of this, indeed, must have been one of the most intense and enduring impressions of Pasternak the poet: he undertook several times to show how a work of art is born.

PASTERNAK AND FUTURISM

Pasternak's connections with Russian futurism have been repeatedly questioned and even denied. In his *Russian Futurism*,

Vladimir Markov supplied not only a careful documentation of Pasternak's actual participation in the futurist group Centrifuge, but succeeded in pinpointing the source of the continued dispute over his futurism.

Markov reached the conclusion that "by 1914 any post-symbolist group with avant-garde aspirations or claims had to join the ranks of domestic futurism." Hence the inevitable characterization of futurism as "flexible, varied, and contradictory."[1] In the light of these conclusions, it becomes evident that the attempts of many critics to disassociate Pasternak from futurism do not always stem from those critics' negative attitudes toward futurism but often result from their definitions of it.

In "Wassermann Test" (1914), Pasternak juxtaposed our technological age, with its leveling tendencies affecting even art and the artists, and those "blessed by-gone times" when individual talent ranked high. The author's preference is obviously for the latter.[2] In "Black Goblet" (1916), he spoke of himself as a futurist, but carefully denied any connection with what he called the "popular" variety of futurism, which saw itself as an expression of the technological age.[3] An attempt to establish what the "true" futurism was and to repudiate the "false" futurism was a characteristic that most futurists shared. By approaching the movement from without and trying to discern its essence behind the gaudy façade, most contemporary critics reduced the diversity of futurism to some unity and thus, inevitably, eliminated many groups and writers from the movement.[4]

Some critics singled out the attention to and interest in contemporary life and the emphasis on language as the elements testifying to the inherent truth of futurism and to the

[1] Vladimir Markov, *Russian Futurism: A History* (Berkeley and Los Angeles: University of California Press, 1968), pp. 240 and 269.

[2] "Vassermanova reakcija," *op.cit.*, p. 33.

[3] *Sočinenija*, III, 147–51.

[4] See, for instance, Fedor Stepun's discussion in "B. L. Pasternak," *Novyj Žurnal*, 56 (March 1959), pp. 187–206.

possibility of its later development. Others spoke of a general tendency of Russian futurism toward primitivism, which manifested itself in the futurists' attempts to discard the culture of the past and to divorce the sound of the word from its meaning. For some, the futurists' urbanism was a transitory feature; for others, their realization of the significance of technology for the twentieth century was the only redeeming feature of the movement. Some critics considered the futurists' emphasis on the purely verbal aspects of poetry, on the "word as such," as rather unimportant, while others attached considerably more significance to it.[5]

These few contemporary opinions suffice to indicate the differences even among those critics who were not dismissing futurism as something insignificant and reducing it to the unconventional behavior of its adherents.

Vladimir Markov, writing from the perspective of the 1950's, rightly considered the urbanism and the rejection of the art of the past as belonging merely to the literary politics of futurism. The essence of futurism, according to him, is in its insistence on the autonomous value of language in poetry: "The idea of futurism is that the word itself creates a new world from within itself, that the word and the world fuse, that the poet penetrates the word."[6] In his book published fourteen years after the article quoted above, Markov is willing to assign more weight to the literary politics of futurism. This, however, does not invalidate his original statement that the essence of futurism is in the fusion of the word and the world. In their approach to poetic language the futurists, according to Markov, were both continuing the approach of the symbolists and at the same time rejecting certain aspects of it.

[5] Valerij Brjusov, "Novye tečenija v russkoj poèzii," *Russkaja Mysl'*, No. 3 (1913), pp. 124–33. Kornej Čukovskij, "Ègo-futuristy i kubo-futuristy," *Šipovnik* (Peterburg), 22 (1914), pp. 97–135. R. V. Ivanov-Razumnik, *Vladimir Majakovskij* ("*Misterija*" ili "*Buff*") (Berlin: Skify, 1922).

[6] Vladimir Markov, "Mysli o russkom futurizme," *Novyj Žurnal*, 38 (1954), p. 174.

That the symbolists attached exceptional significance to poetic language can hardly be disputed. A new development and refinement of poetic means of expression was spoken of by some of them as the primary aim of symbolism. Others sensed in poetic speech the original mystical life of words. For Andrey Bely, poetry was directly concerned with creating language, and poetic language as such was the expression of creativity.[7]

However great the similarity between the symbolists and the futurists in their general preoccupation with poetic speech, the differences in their approach are perhaps even greater. For the symbolists a word stood for something beyond itself; for the futurists it became an end in itself. The word, after being neglected for too long, finally realized its own power and demanded more attention from those who had only recently recognized its autonomous value. As early as 1909 Innokenty Annensky spoke of unrestrained verbal experimentation as a logical and a predictable development.[8]

The understandable demand for attention to the phonetic aspect of language later assumed menacing proportions. Elevating language from a secondary role, futurists were inclined to overstress its importance. In Markov's opinion, the futurist idea of the word's autonomy had an inherent danger of "dehumanizing" the word. Deprived of its symbolist heritage, the idea of the autonomy of language led to a concentration on the purely technological aspects of verbal experimentation.

For Markov, Pasternak is the poet who successfully avoided this "dehumanizing" trend, and in whose work the essential concept of futurism found its best and most complete realization. In his poetry he achieved a fusion of lyrical hero with

---

[7] Andrej Belyj, "Magija slov," *Simvolizm* (Moskva: Musaget, 1910), pp. 429–48. "Brjusov—teoretik simvolizma" (K istorii simvolizma), published with comments by K. Loks in *Literaturnoe Nasledstvo*, 27–28, p. 272. Innokentij Annenskij, "O sovremennom lirizme," *Apollon*, No. 1 (1909), pp. 12–42. See also V. Gofman, "Jazyk simvolistov," *Literaturnoe Nasledstvo*, 27–28, pp. 54–105.

[8] Annenskij, "O sovremennom lirizme," *op.cit.*, p. 21.

45

nature and the word. The assimilation of the third element, the word, into the "poet-nature" formula of romantic poets makes, in Markov's opinion, Pasternak's accomplishment original and illustrates in practice the basic idea of futurism.[9] It is in this sense that Markov speaks in his book of Pasternak's developing "a futurism of his own."

Yury Tynyanov also saw Pasternak's poetry on the one hand as a logical development of the "liberation of the word" accomplished by the futurists and on the other as an extremely successful demonstration of the interrelation of the word and the object. In Pasternak's poetry, says Tynyanov, "the word becomes an almost palpable poetic object."[10]

In his poetic practice Pasternak achieves a synthesis of the futurist attempt to counteract the automatization of poetic language and the symbolist view that poetic language represents the essence of the world perceived intuitively by the poet. In Pasternak's work these two aspects become inseparable.

In his later years Pasternak often commented on his early style. Although such retrospective interpretation is inevitably influenced by the poet's later views, it is invaluable in that it reveals some previously unknown facts and states the aims—regardless of the degree of success of their realization in his poetic practice—that the poet had at the time.

In *Autobiographical Sketch* Pasternak has interpreted the formal complexity of his early style not as an aim in itself but as a substitute for a simplicity that was then still inaccessible. He spoke of the verbal originality of the poets of his generation, including himself, as something forced on them by their own ineptitude. Pasternak does not attempt to disassociate himself from the prevalent tendencies of the times: "At that time my sense of hearing was impaired by the turning and twisting and destroying of everything accepted and usual, [attitudes] which were in vogue those days. Nothing said in a normal way touched me. I forgot that words by themselves, apart from the

[9] Markov, "Mysli o russkom futurizme," *op.cit.*, pp. 176–77.
[10] Jurij Tynjanov, "Promežutok" (O poèzii), in *Arxaisty i novatory* (Leningrad: Priboj, 1929), pp. 541–80. The quotation is on p. 572.

embellishments with which they are decorated, can contain and mean something. ... It was not the essence, but the extraneous piquancy that I looked for in everything."[11] Forgetting that words mean something by themselves implies an undivided attention to phonetics. Pasternak himself provides the answer to the question why—leaving aside the undeniable influence of futurism—his early style was as complex and as original as we know it to be.

In *Safe Conduct*, speaking of his transition from music to poetry, Pasternak touches upon the subject of the verbal originality of his early poems. He traces the source of this originality to a combination of the influence of Bely and Blok and to a peculiar quality of his own mode of expression. This peculiarity of expression resulted, in Pasternak's opinion, from his complete abstinence from writing when he was devoting his time and energy to music—in his own words, "sacrificing word to sound."[12]

Pasternak's retrospective judgments tend to oversimplify the situation. The search for "extraneous piquancy" and concentration on "the embellishments" of words to the detriment of meaning fit into the contemporary scene and are a part of Pasternak's futurism. He is probably just in claiming that the complexity and supposed incomprehensibility of his early style resulted in part from a prolonged abstinence from writing, but it seems that the main cause was the originality of his poetic vision.

Art, according to Pasternak, results from the poet's attempt to name the new aspect of reality revealed to him: "Apart from that ... everything in the world has been named. Only it is unnamed and new. We try to give it a name. The result is art."[13] Giving names to the new that the poet experiences becomes the aim of his work.

Pasternak's perception of his surroundings as if seen for the first time and his depiction of them as if he were trying to name

[11] *Sočinenija*, II, 45.
[12] *Ibid.*, II, 214.
[13] *Ibid.*, II, 241.

them was noticed early. Marina Tsvetaeva emphasized this aspect of Pasternak's poetry in her 1922 article. According to Tsvetaeva, Pasternak does not know "our words" because his world is as young as it was after the Creation. His language is as overwhelming and incomprehensible to us as the language of paradise, savages, and children.[14]

Pasternak's "primitivism"—described by Tsvetaeva as his belonging to the first days of Creation and by Akhmatova as "eternal childhood"[15]—is different from the primitivism attained at the expense of culture. Unlike his contemporaries, who often rejected one at the expense of the other, Pasternak managed to combine a refined culture with a fresh and original perception of nature and life. His path was different both from the "urbanistic" futurism of Mayakovsky and the "primitivistic" futurism of Khlebnikov. Pasternak did not share in his contemporaries' utopian beliefs, whether stemming from a fascination with the technological achievements of the age or from nostalgia for the distant and primitive past.

Unlike a child or a savage who experiences nature directly because he has no distorting screen of civilization before his eyes, the poet penetrates beyond the outward masks of objects and phenomena with the help of poetic inspiration which destroys all obstacles in the path of his vision:

Что в том, что на вселенной—маска?
Что в том, что нет таких широт,
Которым на зиму замазкой
Зажать не вызвались бы рот?

What of it, if the universe is wearing a mask?
What of it, if there are no such latitudes,
That there would not be those who would [volunteer to] gag [them]
With putty [like windowpanes] for winter?

[14] Marina Cvetaeva, "Svetovoj liven'," *Proza* (New York: Chekhov Publishing House, 1953), p. 356.
[15] Anna Axmatova, "Boris Pasternak" (1936), *Sočinenija* (Inter-Language Literary Associates, 1965), I, 224–25.

The objects themselves respond to the poet's inspiration; they
tear off their masks and reveal their true essence:

Но вещи рвут с себя личину,
Теряют власть, роняют честь,
Когда у них есть петь причина,
Когда для ливня повод есть.[16]

But objects tear off their masks,
Lose control, disgrace themselves,
When there is cause for a song,
When there is reason for a downpour.

Pasternak's ability to perceive the new and unexpected
aspects of familiar phenomena is not limited to nature.
Tynyanov speaks of the Pushkin of *Themes and Variations* as
Pushkin not in his standard and long-accepted guise and who
has, as a result, the novel appearance of a "descendant of a
flat-lipped Hamite." "Tearing off the masks" in Pasternak's
poetry is justified, in Tynyanov's opinion, by the unusual,
specific, and "casual" point of view of childhood, illness, etc.
The situations of which Pasternak chooses to speak by their
very nature call attention to the usually nonapparent aspects of
things: the "distorted" view is justified by the condition
itself.[17]

Trying to select one of the most characteristic elements of
Tolstoy's art, Pasternak comes to the conclusion that it was
his unusual originality, which in Pasternak's interpretation
becomes very similar to the effects produced by his own poetic
vision: "All his life, at any given time he [Tolstoy] possessed
an ability to see phenomena in the isolated finality of a
separate moment, in exhaustive and sharp relief, as we see
things only on rare occasions, in childhood, on a crest of
all-renewing happiness, or in the triumph of a great spiritual
victory."[18]

This ability not to succumb to the accepted view of the

[16] *Sočinenija*, I, 86.
[17] Tynjanov, *op.cit.*, p. 564.
[18] *Sočinenija*, II, 28–29.

surroundings and to see the usual as the unusual is one of the most characteristic elements of Pasternak's own art. Giving adequate name to the unusual that the poet perceives is the purpose of his art. Thus the originality of Pasternak's language is the inevitable result of and the function of the poet's new vision of the world. The new objects that surround the poet call for new and unexpected combinations of words and hence the startling juxtapositions of words from various lexical strata in Pasternak's pre-1940 poetry and its extreme syntactic complexity.

In *Safe Conduct*, speaking of his first experience of nature, Pasternak mentions the experience of naming. Finding in the encyclopedia the names of the flowers and plants that he encountered in nature brought him relief and satisfaction, a sense of accomplishment. The same experience is given to the young heroine of "Childhood of Luvers," who is gradually becoming aware of the world around her. As a small child, she wakes up in the middle of the night and sees a delirium-like scene through a window: a card game on the terrace and the lights of a factory in the distance. She is not disturbed by the first, because it has a name known to her, but is frightened by the sight beyond, because it has no name. Although the name does not explain anything to her, the girl is satisfied when she learns it. Names remain her concern throughout the story. At a railroad station her mother approaches "that which was referred to (*названо*) ... as the 'stationmaster.'" [19] The girl is interested neither in the person nor in his position, but only in the name.

Through Zhenya Luvers' experiences, Pasternak comments on the correspondence between the name and the essence of an object. The girl experiences them not as a unity, but separated from each other. On the way from Perm to Ekaterinburg she is fascinated by the expanse of the forest and by what appears to her from a train window as a gigantic and motionless cloud in the distance. She immediately connects the object with its name, because the name "Ural" in her mind corresponded to

[19] *Ibid.*, ii, 83–136. Quotation is on p. 93.

that which she saw; she sensed at once that the region had "a sonorous mountain name." The name was present in the rocks and in the sand scattered in the valley; it was whispered by the trees around the train.

On the same train trip Zhenya lives through another experience of recognizing and naming a phenomenon. While she is waiting for "the frontier of Asia," the image grows to fantastic proportions in her mind. She knows the name and expects to see something striking and is genuinely disappointed when in place of a "geographic tragedy" a rapidly disappearing signpost is pointed out to her. If in the first instance there was an exact correspondence between the staggering view and its name, in the second the perceived aspect of the phenomenon was not adequate to the name, to which she attached a far greater importance. Zhenya is bothered by the lack of visible signs that could prove to her that she is in Asia. She senses that the name should bespeak the essence of a phenomenon. The same concern for finding the correspondence between the object and the name is evident in *Doctor Zhivago*. Lara—whose distant forerunner is Zhenya Luvers—sees the purpose of her life in calling each thing she encounters by its *right* name.[20]

Man gives names to objects not at random but because he recognizes the idea inherent in them; in other words, the name belongs to the named rather than to the one who is naming. The true nature of the word as an organic unity between sound and idea is most adequately realized in poetic speech. Pasternak's poet knows the right names of natural phenomena because he and nature are one; the poet is the spokesman for mute nature. The tremendous task of confining the essence of nature within his lines is accomplished by the poet through the miracle of language.

An early poem "Лесное" ("Sylvan," 1913) is developed around the juxtaposition of the muteness of nature (a forest) and the power of speech of the poet: he speaks for nature.[21]

[20] *Ibid.*, IV, 76.
[21] *Ibid.*, I, 363.

The idea that the search for the true names of things is the purpose of poetry was especially dear to the symbolists, but the belief in the dynamic power of language in general and of poetic language in particular was characteristic of the post-symbolist poets as well.[22]

Contradicting his own statement that in his futurist period his attention was primarily directed toward attaining "extraneous piquancy," in another place in *Autobiographical Sketch* Pasternak insists that *what* a poem said was always of primary concern for him.[23] The idea of the significance of content as an intrinsic part of a work of art is very prominent in *Doctor Zhivago*. In his Varykino journal Zhivago defines art as a mysterious element of content: "I have never seen art as a subject or an aspect of form, but rather as a mysterious and hidden part of content."[24] It is not a simple addition of form to content, but an integration of the two elements that results in an organic unity that is a work of art.

Dependence on his material, on language, does not lead the poet away from life and reality; on the contrary it assures his contact with them because his material by itself possesses meaning.

In 1922 Pasternak wrote that both poetry and artistic prose come face to face with life *in their medium*. Poetry "searches for the melody of nature in the noise of a dictionary," and artistic prose looks for and discovers man in the category of speech.[25]

From the point of view of Pasternak's own ideas about

---

[22] See, for example, Valerij Brjusov, "Karl V," Dialog o realizme v iskusstve, *Zolotoe Runo*, No. 4 (1906), pp. 61–67. Vjačeslav Ivanov, "Zavety simvolizma," *Apollon*, No. 8 (1910), p. 9. Two random examples of the post-symbolist attitude toward language are Nikolaj Gumilev's famous poem "Slovo" (*Sobranie sočinenij v četyrex tomax*, II [Washington: Victor Kamkin, Inc., 1964], p. 39) and Vladimir Majakovskij's "Neo-končennoe" (*Priglušennye golosa*, ed. Vladimir Markov [New York: Chekhov Publishing House, 1952], p. 212).

[23] *Sočinenija*, II, 32.

[24] *Ibid.*, IV, 291.

[25] *Ibid.*, III, 155.

poetic language and their implementation in his work, the years 1917–1918 have to be considered a separate period. Those years were the time when language enjoyed an absolute priority in Pasternak's poetic world. In this connection, the description of the protagonist's process of writing in *A Tale* is very significant: "He ... began to cross out and to scribble over trying to attain the desired vividness. At times he wrote words that did not exist in the language. He would leave them on paper for the time being, hoping that later they would lead him to more direct streams of rain water—to the spoken language that results from the intercourse of ecstasy with the every-day."[26] Two points are of significance here. First, the author's originality is the result of his desire to be more expressive. Secondly, the artist does not attempt to control the language and to adapt it to his needs, but obeys it and expects that language itself will lead him to adequate expression.

Pasternak described his own approach to language during 1917–1918 in a strikingly similar way. In a letter to a Georgian poet, Simon Chikovani (October 1957), he wrote that during those years his approach to the writing of poetry was basically different both from the preceding and the following periods. Whereas at other times he was attracted by what impressed him as "striking, or profound, or fervent, or powerful," during those years his goal was to keep intact the extemporaneous nature of his poems. Pasternak explains that this went beyond attempting to finish a poem in one sitting and consciously avoiding working over his drafts: "During those years ('17 and '18) I wrote down only that which appeared to come to life by itself and to attain unity by its language, by the turn of phrase."[27] Thus during 1917–1918 the principle itself—on which his selection of impressions "which became poems" was based—differed both from the preceding and the following years. Like Serezha in *A Tale*, he was giving himself up to the element of language rather than asserting his own power over

[26] *Ibid.*, ii, 189.
[27] "Kraj, stavšij mne vtoroj rodinoj," *Voprosy Literatury*, No. 1 (1966), p. 199.

it. In abandoning this principle of selection, however, Pasternak did not relegate language to a secondary role.

In *Doctor Zhivago* he asserted the significance of language with respect to all formal aspects of a work of literature. Compared with the years 1917–1918, his view of the part language plays in a work of literature became more subtle and profound: "The dominant thing is no longer the state of mind the artist seeks to express but the language in which he wants to express it. Language, the home and receptacle of beauty and meaning, itself begins to think and speak for man and turns wholly into music, not in terms of sonority but in terms of the impetuousness and power of its inward flow."[28] The laws inherent in the language take over and regulate the whole complexity of the formal aspects of a work of art. This idea is further explicated in Zhivago's Varykino journal, where he speaks of the correlation between the meter and the subject matter of a poem. As an example Zhivago mentions Pushkin's lyceum verse, where he demonstrates a close connection between the length of the line and the theme of a poem.[29]

This principle is illustrated by a detailed description of Zhivago's choosing the meter for his poem "Сказка" ("Fairy Tale"). He begins by using pentameter, but is annoyed by the "false melodiousness" of the meter itself. Changing from a pentameter to a tetrameter is compared to a struggle against verbosity in prose. Shortening the line makes writing more difficult, but at the same time more attractive. In the end Zhivago chooses a trimeter, which proves to be the right meter for this poem: "The words felt crowded in a trimeter; the last traces of his sleepiness disappeared; he felt awake and excited; the right words came, prompted by the brevity of the lines."[30]

[28] *Sočinenija*, iv, 448. Translation by Max Hayward and Manya Harari (New York: Pantheon), p. 437.

[29] *Ibid.*, iv, 293. The interrelation between the meter (trochaic pentameter) of a poem and its theme is analyzed by Kiril Taranovski in "O vzaimootnošenii stixotvornogo ritma i tematiki," *American Contributions to the Fifth International Congress of Slavists* (Mouton, 1963), i, 287–322.

[30] *Sočinenija*, iv, 452.

Creative power is inherent in the material the poet uses; in this case, the chosen meter actively shapes the content.

For Pasternak the sound and the meaning of speech are inseparable and have to be considered together: "I always maintained, as I do now, that the music of poetry is not an acoustic phenomenon and does not consist in the euphony of the vowels and consonants taken by themselves, but in the correlation of the meaning and the sound of speech."[31] This insistence on fusion of sound and meaning in poetic speech decisively sets Pasternak apart from those futurists who in trans-sense language deliberately disregarded the meaning of words.

According to his own assertion, Pasternak did not share the futurists' dream of creating a new language; in his opinion, the overabundance of *what* an artist wants to say should leave him no time for seeking new means of expression. Pasternak extends this thesis to include other arts: he sees the great achievement of both Chopin and Skryabin in their ability to express fascinatingly new content by means that had existed before them.[32]

Among the features that separate Pasternak from the futurists—apart from his fundamentally different view of language as an indissoluble unity of sound and meaning and, on an entirely different level, his inability to go along with their behavior—is his very pronounced and conscious affinity with cultural tradition. Describing his 1912 impressions of Venice, Pasternak speaks of the "palpable unity of our culture."[33] In an article written in 1917 he considers the futurists' rejection of the past as only a transitory stage and finds an excuse for it in their immaturity.[34] Thus Pasternak's divergence from the futurists' rejection of past culture dates

[31] *Ibid.*, II, 25.

[32] *Ibid.*, II, 13. This quality of Skrjabin's art was also pointed out by Boris Asaf'ev in his *Skrjabin. Opyt xarakteristiki* (Peterburg-Berlin: Svetozar, 1923).

[33] *Ibid.*, II, 262–63.

[34] "Kritičeskie ètjudy," *op.cit.*, pp. 18–19.

from at least 1917 and is not a stage he attained by the time of writing *Safe Conduct*. There he wrote that the only response the symbolist art called forth was not a desire to discard it, but to repeat it anew.[35] He does not limit this response to the relationship between his generation and their immediate predecessors. The idea of the continuity of art appears in a more generalized form in *Doctor Zhivago*. In his Varykino journal Zhivago defines the forces at the source of progress in the sciences and in art as rejection and attraction, respectively. Science moves ahead by rejecting mistakes and disproving false theories of predecessors; in art, the example of the predecessors serves as a catalyst for the art of the followers.[36]

Markov maintains that Pasternak's anti-aestheticism, especially that of his second book of verse, *Поверх барьеров* (*Above the Barriers*, 1917), is a characteristic he shares with the futurists.[37] It appears, however, that by using anti-aesthetic imagery and "unpoetic" vocabulary Pasternak was not demonstrating his disregard for the cultural and poetic tradition, nor was he employing it in order to scandalize his readers. Even if we allow for some measure of this feeling in Pasternak before 1917, it can be argued that his anti-aestheticism actually had deeper roots, because for him it was a legitimate and necessary means of expression rather than an end in itself. What underlies Pasternak's anti-aestheticism and is the most important element of his affinity with futurism is the struggle against the automatization of poetic speech.

REALISM OF PASTERNAK

An obvious similarity between the titles of the book of verse (*My Sister, Life*), which early in Pasternak's career established his reputation with the lovers of poetry, and of the novel ("*Doctor Life*"), which thirty-five years later attracted the attention of a world-wide audience, points to an important

---

[35] *Sočinenija*, II, 266–67.

[36] *Ibid.*, IV, 294.

[37] Markov, *Russian Futurism*, p. 270.

aspect of Pasternak's conception of art. During his long career, Pasternak was consistent in emphasizing the significance of real, everyday life for poetry.

In his early poems Pasternak repeatedly pointed out the strong and intimate ties of poetry and the poet with life. In one early poem (1917) the poet "feeds" on the life around him. He dissolves in life, his blood cells rush into life so as to collect and bring back to the poet particles of life:

Сколько жадных моих кровинок
В крови облаков, и помоев, и будней
Ползут в эти поры домой, приблудные,
Снедь жизни, снедь тайны оттаявшей вынюхав.[38]

And how many of my avid blood cells
In the blood of the clouds, and in slops, and everyday
    drudgery
At this hour crawl home, the stray ones,
Having sniffed out the feed of life, the feed of thawed-out
    mystery.

The process of absorbing from his surroundings goes on incessantly in the poet's life; it is a permanent aspect of his existence as a poet.

In an often-quoted poem in *Above the Barriers* (1917), the poet implores poetry to cling to life and to take in everything that comes within its reach:

Поэзия! Греческой губкой в присосках
Будь ты, и меж зелени клейкой
Тебя б положил я на мокрую доску
Зеленой садовой скамейки.

Расти себе пышные брыжжи и фижмы,
Вбирай облака и овраги,
А ночью, поэзия, я тебя выжму
Во здравие жадной бумаги.[39]

[38] *Stixotvorenija*, p. 513.
[39] *Sočinenija*, I, 202.

Poetry! Be a Greek sponge covered with tendrils,
And amid the young sticky greenery
I will place you on a wet board
Of a green garden bench.

Grow for yourself luxuriant flounces and farthingales
Take in clouds and ravines,
And at night, O poetry, I will squeeze you out
For the good of the thirsty paper.

The image of poetry as a sponge imbibing impressions from life reappears in the 1922 article "A Few Principles": to attain to the level where it would be able to contribute to life, poetry has first to enrich itself by the process of assimilation from life.[40]

In his assertions of poetry's dependence on real life, Pasternak goes beyond the repetition of the self-evident and undeniable truth that all art ultimately has its roots in life. He not only insists on the everyday quality of occurrences that inspire the poet, but actually declares that life with its minute details *is* poetry. In "Поэзия" ("Poetry," 1922), defining poetry, the poet rejects the grandiose and the pretentious for the inconspicuous and the insignificant:

Ты не осанка сладкогласца,
Ты—лето с местом в третьем классе,
Ты—пригород, а не припев.

You are not the pose of a mellifluous man,
You are a summer with a third-class ticket,
You are a suburb, not a refrain.

The poet does not fear the self-evident truths and the commonplace in poetry:

Поэзия, когда под краном
Пустой, как цинк ведра, трюизм,
То и тогда струя сохранна,
Тетрадь подставлена—струись![41]

[40] *Ibid.*, III, 152.
[41] *Ibid.*, I, 101.

It is poetry, when there is an empty truism
Under the faucet, like a tin pail,
Even then the flow is preserved,
The notebook is ready—pour!

In the fifties, Pasternak wrote that his fascination with the simple and the everyday and his innate ability to perceive the ordinary manifestations of life as exceptional precluded any interest on his part in the fantastic and the bizarre as such.[42]

In a chapter of his memoirs published in 1966, Veniamin Kaverin refers to his correspondence with Pasternak on the subject of the abstract and the concrete in art. In this correspondence, which apparently took place in the late 1920's, Kaverin defended the right of art to be free from everyday reality, whereas Pasternak opposed abstraction in literature and insisted on the interrelation of poetry and everyday prose.[43] Emphasizing this point in his speech at the first All-Union Congress of Writers in 1934, Pasternak arrived at a paradoxical definition of poetry as prose, where prose stands for everyday actuality and poetry for its voice.[44]

In *Safe Conduct* Pasternak wrote that an artist re-creates what his poetic vision allows him to discern in the real world. Every "new" and "original" metaphor is not the invention of a poet but a partial uncovering of the truth about the world, and, therefore, implicitly, "realistic": "[Art] is realistic in that it did not invent metaphor by itself, but discovered it in nature and reproduced it faithfully."[45] From this it follows that artistic creativity is discovering and revealing to the world that which is inherent in the cosmos but which cannot be perceived without the help of artistic vision. Something that was *always* there is revealed *now* through the creative inspiration of an artist. This view places art on a par with science: just as scientific dis-

---

[42] Jacqueline de Proyart, *Pasternak* (Paris: Editions Gallimard, 1964). p. 238.

[43] V. Kaverin, "Neskol'ko let," *Novyj Mir*, No. 11 (1966), pp. 132–58.

[44] *Sočinenija*, III, 217.

[45] *Ibid.*, II, 243.

coveries reveal the ever-existing laws of nature, so artistic creativity unveils the eternal beauty of the world. What science and art discover is in existence, irrespective of man's knowledge of it.

Pasternak stresses that art is connected with reality in the closest and most intricate of ways. It depends on reality and is inconceivable without it. He expressed this quite unambiguously in "A Few Principles." Art has always existed alongside life, and therefore one cannot speak of its beginning or end. This conception de-emphasizes—if not eliminates entirely—the "artificial" aspect of art: art is not the superfluous product of fantasy but an essential corollary of life. On this assumption are based all of Pasternak's later statements about realism in art.

In the same article he affirms the value of creative imagination in most categorical terms. The world itself is the only successful creation of imagination: "The real living world is the only 'conception' of imagination that succeeded once and continues being successful without end. It lasts and is victorious every moment. It still is real, profound, and astonishingly fascinating. One does not get disappointed in it the next morning. For a poet it serves more as an example than as a model." [46] This statement suggests that artistic creativity is not based so much on imitation of reality as on continuation of it: man's creativity continues the creation of the world.

This essentially romantic conception does not lead Pasternak away from reality. On the contrary, an artist succeeds not by resisting or avoiding life but by giving in to it. The extraordinary power of the art of the poet-improvisator in *A Tale* stems from his "complete and unconditional" subjugation to life.[47] In the first poem of the cycle "Художник" ("The Artist," 1936) an artist's organic ties with life are stressed; he is sustained by life itself: "Как поселенье на Гольфштреме, / Он создан весь земным теплом."[48] ("Like a settlement on

[46] *Ibid.*, ɪɪɪ, 155.
[47] *Ibid.*, ɪɪ, 192.
[48] *Ibid.*, ɪɪɪ, 3.

the Gulf Stream, / He is created entirely by the warmth of the earth.")

In the forties Pasternak attempted a more precise formulation of his views on the subject of realism. In this respect his articles on Verlaine and Chopin, published in 1944 and 1945, respectively, are of great import. Here as elsewhere, Pasternak consistently avoids accepted definitions and classifications: he is not concerned with realism as a literary movement or school. This is in complete accord with his earlier views. In "Letters from Tula" (1918) a true artistic achievement is demonstrated to be independent of realistic detail. In the story the only one who succeeds in attaining the level of true art is an old actor who re-enacts a scene without anything in his physical environment to support him. On the other hand, a cinematographic group that aims at a precise reproduction of a historical setting and is aided by the most elaborate realistic props fails: despite the group's "realism" it does not attain true art.[49]

A similarly negative attitude toward "realism" based on meaningless accumulation of facts is found in *Doctor Zhivago*. Although the attack in this case is specifically directed against war correspondents, the implications of Zhivago's statements are more general. True facts as such have no relation to art. Without the intervention of human creativity, collecting of facts is meaningless, and the resulting "realism" has little relation either to true art or to true life.[50]

In his Chopin article, which he considered very important for his views on art, Pasternak defined realism as a "degree of art." Realism, according to him, is the highest level of precision and detailing that can be demanded only by the artist himself. For Pasternak there are two elements essential in forming a realist artist: impressibility early in life and conscientiousness during his mature years. These two force the artist to work and to achieve that level of precision which is realism.[51] By implication, a true realist is not free, because he follows life rather than his own whims.

[49] *Ibid.*, II, 75–82.   [50] *Ibid.*, IV, 123–24.
[51] *Ibid.*, III, 171–75.

Applying this definition of realism, Pasternak classifies as realists Verlaine and Blok, Chopin and Skryabin. Modern art, in Pasternak's opinion, was brought to life by the new reality of the second half of the nineteenth century. The new urban civilization pointed to the coming changes; reality itself was symbolic. By striving to depict it truthfully, the artists became symbolists. According to Pasternak, they were the true realists, because they faithfully reproduced the new reality that was different from the reality of a Pushkin or a Balzac.[52]

Being true to the reality of the times is the highest praise Pasternak offers other artists. It is also the quality that invariably attracts him. Thus, for instance, one of the outstanding characteristics of Skryabin's music was, in Pasternak's opinion, its absolute adequacy to the time when it was written: "[In Skryabin's music] everything is contemporary, everything is full of inner correspondences, expressible by music, with the surrounding external world, with the way in which at that time people lived, thought, felt, traveled, dressed."[53] Likewise, Blok's sensitivity and acute perception of surrounding life brought reality into his poetry. This is why his Petersburg, says Pasternak, is the most real Petersburg in modern art. It is permeated with everyday prose and exists without distinction both in real life and in the poet's imagination.

It is clear that both during his early and late period, Pasternak's definition of realism was highly idiosyncratic. His frequent return to the subject indicates that the poet placed great store in emphasizing the divergence of his "realism" from the accepted interpretation of the term. The use of the word itself in his later articles, as well as his insistence that his own art was rooted in reality, perhaps were the poet's attempts, albeit naive, to defend himself from the perennial accusations of "divorce from reality."

In *Autobiographical Sketch*, discussing the importance of Blok's influence on himself and other poets of his generation, Pasternak singles out the theme of the big city in Blok's poetry.

[52] *Ibid.*, III, 168–71.
[53] *Ibid.*, II, 13.

Pasternak sees the big city not only as the main protagonist of Blok's poetry, but as an essential element of his biography as a poet.[54] Pasternak's own relationship to the city is rather complex. For the young Pasternak, the city was something that stood apart from his life, something he was viewing from a distance. In *Safe Conduct* Pasternak characterized the essence of city life as the opposite of creativity: heaviness and inertia are its basic elements; it is static and entirely devoid of spirituality and dynamism.

Although urban imagery plays a significant role in Pasternak's early poetry (especially in *Above the Barriers*, 1917), there is no doubt that it is not the city but nature that attracts him. Even his poems with an urban setting are full of rains, storms, trees, and stars. This tendency is even stronger in his late work. Yury Zhivago moves from Moscow to the Urals, from a city to a more primitive environment. He and Lara escape from Yuryatin and civilization to the snowy desert of Varykino.

Pasternak's natural predilection notwithstanding, he repeatedly stresses his awareness of the role of urban civilization in the life of twentieth-century man. If in Pasternak's early work the city appears as the inevitable setting of contemporary life, and thus its significance is acknowledged by implication, in his later work it is affirmed repeatedly and explicitly. In a poem from 1931 the poet specifically connects his destiny with Moscow and twentieth-century urban civilization.[55] When Zhivago discovers the joy of physical work and opposes his healthy and more primitive life during his first Varykino stay to that of life in the city, he emphasizes that he does not follow Tolstoy in his denunciation of civilization. He explains that in his case the escape was caused by special circumstances and attracted him as a relatively freer existence.

Zhivago repeats Pasternak's view that externally chaotic new art reflects the new urban reality. He speaks of the present-day city in general and of post-revolutionary Moscow in particular

[54] *Ibid.*, ii, 16.
[55] *Ibid.*, i, 321.

63

as the only source and inspiration of truly contemporary art. In the epilogue of the novel, Moscow is spoken of not only as the site where Zhivago had lived, but as the subject matter and the heroine of his work.[56] It is not accidental that Zhivago, like Pasternak himself, left more statements on the significance of the city in modern life and art than poems specifically about the city. It is suggested in the novel that Zhivago's only poem that might be connected with the urban theme is "Hamlet," but the "big city" is one of the prominent themes of the novel, and the city-scape serves as the background for many of Zhivago's poems.[57]

In two poems of Pasternak's later period his contradictory attitude toward the big city and everything it stands for is very clear. In the poem "Город" ("City," 1941) the poet admits that in his "childish dreams" the city took the place of heaven. From afar it appears attractive even now: its innumerable comforts are contrasted to the primitive way of life in the countryside in wintertime.[58] In the poem "Поездка" ("A Journey," 1958) the poet again views the city from afar. It might be a reminiscence of an earlier longer poem, "City," which was originally written in 1916 and considerably reworked and extended in 1928.[59] In both poems the poet is on a train. In the earlier poem a kaleidoscopic picture of the approaches to the city conveys both the speed of the express-train and the complexity and diversity of the city itself. In the 1958 poem, to the sensation of motion is opposed the unchanging forest seen from the train. The city is designated as the place where passions are at play in the name of "reshaping of the world"[60] which for Pasternak stands for betrayal of life itself. Present-day urban civilization as such is not judged as good or bad; the

[56] *Ibid.*, IV, 286–87, 500, 530.

[57] This aspect of the Živago poems is examined by D. D. Obolenskij in "Stixi Doktora Živago," *Sbornik statej, posvjaščennyx tvorčestvu B. L. Pasternaka* (München, 1962), pp. 103–14.

[58] *Sočinenija*, III, 24–25.

[59] *Ibid.*, I, 240–43, 477.

[60] *Ibid.*, III, 103–104.

uses to which man puts it determine its value. Clearly, Pasternak had moved far from his youthful rejection of the technological age (see p. 43, above), a rejection which, however, was not replaced with fascination but with a rather matter-of-fact acceptance.

For Pasternak as a poet of the post-symbolist period, the reality of urban civilization was an inherent element of contemporary art. Zhivago dismisses "pastoral simplicity" in present-day literature as a forgery that deliberately overlooks the reality of the technological age. Zhivago's statement might be Pasternak's reply to some of his critics, who saw the interrelation of the city and nature in his poetry as proof that his experiences of nature did not go beyond the experiences of a city dweller at his дача, that he was not able to escape petty household imagery even in his nature poems.[61] Other critics sensed Pasternak's desire to integrate the two elements and considered his achievement a success.[62]

It appears that Pasternak attempted a new synthesis of nature and urban civilization in his poetry; he refused to reject one at the expense of the other. His fundamental attraction is to nature, but he brings with him not only the everyday physical environment of a city dweller, but—as Sinyavsky correctly notes—his social and historical associations as well.[63] All those elements have a legitimate place in his poetry; he succeeds in retaining freshness of vision without any impairment to culture or civilization.

This search for a solution different from those presented by the framework of Russian culture was perhaps one of the decisive factors behind Pasternak's instant and very strong attraction to Georgia. D. Mirsky, in an article on Pasternak's translations of Georgian poetry, pointed out that the contemporary Georgian poets managed to preserve a natural freshness

[61] See, for instance, Valerian Pravduxin, "V bor'be za novoe iskusstvo," *Sibirskie Ogni*, No. 5 (1922), pp. 174–81; and Kornelij Zelinskij, "Liričeskaja tetrad'," *God Šestnadcatyj*, No. 1 (1933), pp. 391–407.

[62] Obolenskij, *op.cit.*, p. 104.

[63] *Stixotvorenija*, p. 37.

65

that Russian poetry had lacked since the middle of the nineteenth century. This natural freshness of the Georgians, however, is not connected with the naiveté or "bad simplicity" often characteristic of the younger literatures.[64]

In March of 1959, in the last of his published letters to his Georgian friends, Pasternak tried to define that "fundamental and elusive" feature of Georgian life and culture that captivated him at the time of his first encounter with that country and that never ceased to fascinate him. When attempting this before, Pasternak had spoken of the strong cultural tradition that enabled the Georgians to keep hold of reality; in 1959 Pasternak described it as the result of the interrelation of contemporary city life and nature.[65] The same qualities Pasternak discerned in Poland. In "Трава и камни" ("Grass and Stones"), a poem written in 1956, the two are placed together:

С действительностью иллюзию,
С растительностью гранит
Так сблизили Польша и Грузия,
Что это обеих роднит.[66]

Illusion and reality,
Granite and vegetation
Have been so closely brought together in Poland
    and Georgia,
That the two become related through this.

Grass is growing in the cracks and crevices of the old walls—nature and civilization exist side by side, neither is replacing the other. Nor does new life destroy the past; Poland and Georgia are able to preserve tradition without becoming ossified. Pasternak praises the ability to build the new without destroying the old, to connect the past with the future. It is easy to discern a reaction against the unfortunate Russian practice of either denigrating the past or becoming uncritically attached

[64] D. Mirskij, "Pasternak i gruzinskie poèty," *Literaturnaja Gazeta*, October 24, 1935.
[65] *Sočinenija*, II, 48–49; and "Kraj, stavšij ...," *op.cit.*, pp. 173, 199–200.
[66] *Sočinenija*, III, 79.

to it and rejecting the new. Quite prominent in the nineteenth-century cultural and literary tradition, this regrettable attitude —in both its forms—grew to abnormal proportions in post-revolutionary times. In attempting a synthesis of nature and civilization in his poetry, Pasternak implicitly attacks the opposition of tradition and progress, of nature and civilization, as the only available alternatives.

A poet's language is, undoubtedly, an immediate expression of his ties with contemporary reality. Pasternak's change from the extreme complexity of his early style to the austere simplicity of his late (post-1940) verse is one of the fundamental problems of his development as a poet. Suffice it to say here that it was a long process and that the causes of this change were both internal and external.[67] It was determined both by the intrinsic features of the poet's temperament and by the literary climate in which he worked. Among the most prominent features of the literary climate affecting Pasternak were cultural conditions in the country and the demands of the party ideologues for realism and accessibility to the masses.

The firmly entrenched nineteenth-century tradition of expecting literature to act as a teacher and guide, combined with the enormous numerical increase of the reading public and, as a consequence, a preponderance of a rather unsophisticated literary taste among the majority of the readers, facilitated the utilization of literature by the party.

Pasternak was very much aware of the enormous lowering of cultural standards and literary tastes, not only among the reading public but among contemporary men of letters as well. In a letter to Simon Chikovani, written in 1957, he praises highly Chikovani's article about the poetry of Titian Tabidze, but pessimistically suggests that Chikovani's subtlety and sophistication will be lost on his audience.[68] Pasternak's alienation from current literary life—frequent references to which abound in his letters—should at least in part be attributed to this ever-widening cultural gap.

[67] This problem is the subject of a separate study of mine (in progress).
[68] "Kraj, stavšij...," *op.cit.*, p. 199.

67

At the same time, without condoning existing cultural conditions, Pasternak accepted them as a reality. Writing in a manner and style not accessible to the masses, a writer forfeits the possibility of reaching them. Pasternak's desire to attain a simple style could have been caused in part by his wish to reach a wider audience. His translation projects—besides solving very real financial problems—served the same purpose. Translations of the European classics not only provided Pasternak with the widest possible audience and gave him a chance to express his own views, even if indirectly,[69] but contributed toward the cultural enlightenment of his audience and served as a laboratory of his new style.

Pasternak's awareness of the party pressure for conformity—often disguised as "accessibility to the masses"—should not be overlooked in this connection. His poetry was repeatedly and consistently condemned as "anti-democratic" for its complex and not easily comprehensible language.[70] To one of his Western visitors, Pasternak mentioned the important work of "literary education" going on in the Soviet Union. This process changed him from an "esoteric poet" to a realist—not a socialist realist, however, as he was careful to point out.[71]

It is hardly necessary to argue that the realism that Pasternak talks about and considers a foundation of his own art is neither the traditional nineteenth-century realism nor the twentieth-century domestic variety known as socialist realism. For Pasternak, to be realistic art has to be truthful to life; this does not imply, however, that art has to follow the methods of the realist school.

One area where Pasternak's definition of realism is very close to the traditional definition of realism is that of language. The simple and unadorned style of late Pasternak tries to reproduce the natural word order of contemporary spoken Russian, and magnificently succeeds in the effort.

[69] Vladimir Markov, "An Unnoticed Aspect of Pasternak's Translations," *Slavic Review*, xx, No. 3 (October, 1961), pp. 503–08.

[70] See *Literaturnaja Gazeta*, February 26, March 5, and May 30, 1937.

[71] Gerd Ruge, "A Visit to Pasternak," *Encounter*, 54 (March 1958), p. 24.

In connection with Blok, Pasternak spoke of the everyday colloquial language that renovates the language of poetry.[72] In his article on Verlaine he emphasized the role of spoken language in modern poetry. As Verlaine's particular achievement Pasternak singled out his introduction of the undistorted syntax of spoken French into lyric poetry. Pasternak praised Verlaine's "unlimited freedom of language" that before could be found only in prose dialogue: "For him turns of speech of French language were indivisible. He wrote using not words, but whole phrases; he did not break them up and did not change the word order."[73] These observations are important for Pasternak's own poetic language. In his later verse there can be found many expressions and phrases of spoken language without any change in the normal word order. Here only a few examples of colloquial expressions or whole sentences of spoken Russian used without inversion are given: "Зимой в деревне нет житья," "Он приходил в себя урывками, / Осматривался на пригорке / И щупал место под нашивками / На почерневшей гимнастерке," "В детстве, я как сейчас еще помню, / Высунешься, бывало, в окно," "Вдруг кто-то вспомнил, что сегодня / Шестое августа по старому, / Преображение Господне."[74] The retention of the original word order is even more obvious in the inclusion of proverbs or sayings: "Расстраиваться не надо: / у страха глаза велики," "Будь, что будет, все равно," "Жизнь прожить—не поле перейти."[75]

Preservation of the normal word order of spoken Russian is undoubtedly a very significant feature of the stylistic simplicity of Pasternak's later works. However, it should not overshadow other more subtle uses of language within the framework of syntactic simplicity. Modifications of traditional word combinations can serve as an example. In "Рассвет" ("Dawn"),[76]

[72] *Sočinenija*, ii, 16.

[73] *Ibid.*, iii, 171.

[74] *Ibid.*, iii, 25, 47, 104; iv, 548. No translation of these examples is attempted, because it is the word order that imparts to them the quality of spoken Russian.

[75] *Ibid.*, iii, 23, 107; iv, 532.

[76] *Ibid.*, iv, 557.

a poem of the Zhivago cycle, only one element of *Новый Завет* (*New Testament*)—the key word *завет*—is retained. It is modified by *твой* instead of the usual *новый* (new) or *ветхий* (old). After introducing the word *завет* the poet proceeds to tell what effect the reading of the Gospels produced on him. Thus the traditional expression and the associations it evokes are by-passed for the depiction of the results the poet's redis- covery of the Gospels brings about. His experience of com- munion with other people is presented as a unique discovery of his own rather than as an expected and predictable consequence.

In "Земля" ("The Earth"),[77] another of Zhivago's poems, the Last Supper is depicted without resorting to this combina- tion of words. First the time is set as early spring in Russia (stanzas one through three); then the participation of cosmic forces in human suffering is indicated (stanza four). The two elements are brought together: an early spring becomes creation's search for fulfillment (stanza five); the idea of redemption is brought in (stanza six). The last stanza (seven) describes a gathering of friends in early spring for an evening feast. The description is in very contemporary, prosaic, every- day language. Both the ideas of leave-taking (*прощанья*) and testament or last will (*завещанья*) are present. The final two lines of the poem—without naming Christ—return to the idea of His suffering for the redemption of man. The expression for Last Supper in Russian—the Church Slavic *Тайная Вечеря*— does not appear as such in the poem, but both words—one in a somewhat modified form—are present. *Вечеря* (evening meal) appears as *вечера* (evening gatherings) in line three of the last stanza, and the word *тайная* in line five. The presence of these words emphasizes the reference.

The effect is similar to that produced by the poem "Dawn." By depicting the event itself and the meaning of it, rather than referring to it by its traditional name, the poet conveys his original experience. The identifying-associating process is reversed: instead of identifying the usual word combination

---

[77] *Ibid.*, IV, 559–60.

that would call forth the traditional associations, the reader is forced to grasp the essence of the occurrence and only then— provided he is aware of it—to associate it with the traditional expression.[78]

Essentially, these examples demonstrate yet another instance of Pasternak's unique ability to see the familiar as something never before seen or experienced, and they are a part of his successful struggle against the automatization of perception.

When *Doctor Zhivago* was published, many critics in the West attempted to relate the novel to the nineteenth-century novelistic tradition.[79] Pasternak's answers to queries on this point further clarify his conception of realism. In Pasternak's view, for the nineteenth-century realists causality was the basic feature of reality they were depicting: "... the belief that the objectivity was determined and ruled by an iron chain of causes and effects, that all appearances of the moral and material world were subordinate to the law of sequels and retributions."[80] According to the author, in his novel he consciously tried to get away from the idea of causality, because for him the essence of reality was in the multiplicity of the universe, in the unlimited number of possibilities rather than in necessity.[81]

In the novel, Pasternak attempted to depict reality as he experienced it, with the emphasis on freedom of choice and on a feeling of reality as a whole: "There is an effort in the novel to represent the whole sequence of facts and beings and

[78] The reason Pasternak avoided the traditional expressions here may well have been extra-literary. I think it can be regarded as a camouflage for the purposes of censorship. If this is so, he was right, for both "Rassvet" and "Zemlja" have been published in the Soviet Union (*Stixotvorenija*, pp. 690–92), whereas those of Živago's poems where Christian themes are presented overtly have not.

[79] This question was fully analyzed by Gleb Struve in "Sense and Nonsense about *Doctor Zhivago*," published in *Studies in Russian and Polish Literatures in Honor of Wacław Lednicki*, ed. Z. Folejewski (Mouton, 1962), pp. 229–50.

[80] "Three Letters to Stephen Spender," *Encounter*, 83 (August 1960), pp. 3–6. Original in English. Quotation appears on p. 4.

[81] Ralph Matlaw, "A Visit with Pasternak," *Nation*, September 12, 1959, pp. 134–35.

happenings like some moving entireness, like a developing, passing by, rolling, and rushing inspiration, as if reality itself had freedom and choice and was composing itself out of numberless variants and versions."[82] In Pasternak's own words, this is the source of the novel's basic difference from the nineteenth-century realistic tradition, manifested in the insufficient delineation of characters and the abundance of coincidences.

In the novel, the ability to respond to ever-changing reality is the standard against which individuals as well as ideologies and political systems are measured. It goes without saying that in an artist this is not only a desirable but an indispensable quality.

Pasternak's realism does share some elements with traditional realism; foremost among them is the contemporary colloquial language and the ordinary, everyday settings of his poems. What the lyrical hero experiences, however, in those ordinary circumstances and what the poet conveys in the present-day spoken language, can hardly be described as ordinary: the poet's fascination with life in its everyday manifestations.

THE GENESIS OF A WORK OF ART

Pasternak illustrated his ideas on the close ties between art and reality by describing how a work of art comes to life. Before *Doctor Zhivago*, he gave a rather detailed account of the genesis of a work of art in *A Tale* (1929),[83] where Serezha, the protagonist, begins to write a story (thus the title applies both to Pasternak's and to the protagonist's work). The first mention of the story precedes and brings about its conception. The protagonist tells an editor, whom he meets by chance, that he is working on a new story. Lack of any previous planning on the author's part is stressed. He had not planned to mention the nonexistent story and was not compelled to do it; he did it quite impulsively.

[82] "Three Letters to Stephen Spender," *op.cit.*, p. 5.
[83] *Sočinenija*, II, 151–202.

During the weeks that follow his conversation with the editor, Serezha is preoccupied with the plight of a young woman who is employed as *une dame de compagnie* in the same household where he serves as a tutor. Because of her financial circumstances, Anna, a cultured woman, has to put up with constant mistreatment by her employer. Pained by his desire and inability to help her, Serezha begins to think of Anna's problem on a universal scale: he needs extraordinary wealth to help all the wronged women of the world. The urgency of the problem is enhanced for Serezha by his encounters with prostitutes: his millions will help all of them and in this way a complete and painless renovation of the world will be achieved.

Soon, the unattainable millions of Serezha's imagination are replaced by a much more realistic two hundred rubles. He recollects his meeting with the Petersburg editor early in the summer and realizes that his still nonexistent story can bring a modest sum of money. He immediately begins a letter to the editor, interrupts himself in order to see Anna, and on the spur of the moment declares his love and proposes marriage to her. As usual with Pasternak's poets, the emotional outburst is followed by a creative one: Serezha returns to his interrupted letter to the editor and to the summary of the story, which by now has been transformed into a drama in verse.

Unlike Raskolnikov, whose name comes to his mind, Serezha commits no crime. His desire for immense wealth, brought about by his compassion for the suffering women, is resolved in his creative activity: his idea attains a poetic incarnation in his unfinished story.

Like Serezha himself, the protagonist of his work is a creative artist preoccupied with the same ideas about the suffering women of the world. Unlike Serezha, however, he not only has a definite plan for the acquisition of wealth, but even succeeds in carrying it out. The improbable situation in Serezha's story of a man auctioning himself off has as a starting point a very real experience on the part of the author: the need of money to help Anna out of her humiliating position.

73

Pasternak returns to a depiction of the genesis of a work of art in *Doctor Zhivago*. Although Serezha's work in *A Tale* is not finished, and the parts included in *A Tale* are described not as the actual work of the protagonist but only as a summary of it, it is an attempt to show how a poetic work is interrelated with its author's life; in this respect, *A Tale* has to be considered as the forerunner of *Doctor Zhivago*. Zhivago, undoubtedly, is a more accomplished poet than the Serezha of *A Tale*; whereas the story recounts the events of a part of one summer, the novel encompasses the entire life of the poet (twenty-five poems included in the novel provide a factual justification of Zhivago's life as a poet).

The relationship between Zhivago's poems and his thoughts and experiences depicted in the novel is obvious in some instances and rather tenuous in others.[84] Two poems, the genesis of which is easily discernible and serves as a further elucidation of Pasternak's view of the interrelation of art and reality, are "Fairy Tale" and "Разлука" ("Parting").

When Zhivago sees Lara for the first time, she is with Komarovsky. What strikes him most is the girl's obvious "enslavement" by the man. Lara is referred to as "a puppet obedient to every movement of [her master's] hand."[85] In the eyes of the young Zhivago this scene has something magic and frightening about it. These first impressions of Lara enslaved

---

[84] The interrelation of Živago's poems and the prose narrative has been analyzed by D. D. Obolenskij (*op.cit.*). Specific connections between the two have been pointed out by George Katkov in his notes to Henry Kamen's translations of Pasternak's late poems (*In the Interlude—Poems 1945–1960* [Oxford: Oxford University Press, 1962]). Unlike Obolenskij and Katkov, who do not attempt to tie all the Živago poems with specific episodes in the text of the prose narrative, another commentator, Donald Davie, tries to do just that. Some of the connections established in his commentary seem to be rather farfetched (*The Poems of Dr. Zhivago* [Manchester University Press, 1965]). An interesting interpretation of the poems within the general framework of the novel is provided by Mary F. Rowland and Paul Rowland in *Pasternak's Doctor Zhivago* (Carbondale: Southern Illinois University Press, 1967).

[85] *Sočinenija*, IV, 61.

by Komarovsky have to be considered the original source of the poem that Zhivago writes many years later. The image of a dragon—pivotal for the poem—appears in the novel long before the writing of the poem and not specifically connected with Komarovsky or even Zhivago. A waterfall that dominates the area where Vasya Brykin escapes from the train is referred to as "a living and conscious creature, a fairytale dragon or a winged serpent." Perhaps it is the same waterfall that Zhivago hears in his sleep during the same night.[86]

Several years later, attempting to calm the upset Lara after Komarovsky's sudden appearance in Yuryatin, Zhivago suggests that he will kill Komarovsky in order to free Lara from her fear.[87] Although obviously an exaggeration and a turn of speech, the suggestion, coming from Zhivago, who tried not to kill even on a battlefield, is surprising. However, if Komarovsky is seen as a dragon who enslaved Lara (Zhivago's first impression of him), then Zhivago is assuming the function of his patron saint St. George, the dragon-slayer, and the suggestion is not as unreasonable as it sounds at first. Likewise, when Zhivago sees the wolves that appear in Varykino one night, the idea of an imminent danger for Lara and himself comes to his mind. The wolves are on his mind during the following day, and, in the end, they are transformed into a dragon: "The wolves he had been remembering all day long were no longer wolves on the snowy plain under the moon, they had become a theme, they had come to symbolize a hostile force bent upon destroying him and Lara and on driving them from Varykino. The thought of this hostility developed in him and by evening it loomed like a prehistoric beast or some fabulous monster, a dragon whose tracks had been discovered in the ravine and who thirsted for his blood and lusted after Lara."[88] During that night he writes the poem about St. George and the dragon. Zhivago's forebodings reflect upon his and Lara's desperate

[86] *Ibid.*, IV, 241–43.
[87] *Ibid.*, IV, 430.
[88] *Ibid.*, IV, 451. Translated by Max Hayward and Manya Harari, p. 440.

situation in Varykino and foretell the return of Komarovsky, the evil genius for both Lara and Zhivago.[89]

Both the work of the protagonist of *A Tale* and the poem "Fairy Tale" have as their origin their respective authors' real-life experiences in meeting endangered or humiliated women in need of help. In Serezha's work the poet manages to carry out his plan—which, however, backfires in the end. In "Fairy Tale," although the knight kills the dragon, his victory is not clear-cut: both he and the maiden are left between life and death. The actions of Serezha and Zhivago do not even go that far; they are different from those depicted in their works: Serezha parts with Anna with surprising ease; Zhivago helps Komarovsky persuade Lara to leave him.

Zhivago's decision to stay in Varykino after Lara's departure is motivated by his desire to write about her. This is the only tangible tribute to Lara of which he is capable. Although Zhivago's desire was to depict Lara precisely as she was, as he knew and remembered her, in the process of writing, without his conscious effort, the real Lara was gradually disappearing. By eliminating everything obviously personal, Zhivago was changing the specific of his personal experiences into the general and the universal.

One of the poems written at that time was "Parting." It is known now that the disorder in the Varykino house and the circumstances of Lara's departure from it, which are depicted in the poem, are connected not only with the life of Zhivago but with the life of Pasternak as well.[90]

Although biographical verisimilitude as such neither adds to nor detracts from a work of art, in the case of the Zhivago poems Pasternak's indication of the connections between some

[89] *Ibid.*, IV, 409–11. On the symbolic significance of the dragon image, see Rowland and Rowland, *op.cit.*

[90] *Sočinenija*, IV, 463–65. Both Hélène Peltier-Zamoyska and George Katkov speak of the poem "Razluka" as depicting the circumstances of the arrest of Pasternak's close personal friend, Olga Ivinskaja, in 1948 (Hélène Peltier-Zamoyska, "Pasternak, homme du passé?" *Esprit*, XXXI, No. 1 [January 1963], note on pp. 19–20; George Katkov, *op.cit.*, pp. 127–28).

poems and specific incidents in Zhivago's life not only supports Zhivago's authorship but emphasizes the significance that Pasternak attached to the interrelation of art and reality. The organic ties of art and reality assure its truthfulness. "Being true to life" is one of the strongest and most consistent sentiments present in Pasternak's work. In 1922 ("A Few Principles") he wrote: "Inability to find and to tell the truth is a shortcoming which cannot be compensated by any amount of skill to tell the untruth."[91]

In his comments on the 1925 party resolution on literature,[92] Pasternak objected to its "unfaithfulness to reality." Pasternak challenged the resolution on three points, all of which were concerned with the disregard for facts rather than with the party ideology or its interference in literary matters. What Pasternak rejected was a presentation of the desired as the already attained and the treating of the undesirable as nonexistent. In the eyes of Pasternak, this approach was a transgression against reality and life that no ideology could redeem.

[91] *Sočinenija*, III, 153.

[92] *Ibid.*, III, 157–59. The resolution of the Central Committee of the Communist Party on literature (June 1925) reaffirmed the basic principle of party control of literature, but disassociated itself from the specific factions, which, at that time, meant curbing the militant proletarian groups and by the same token allowing relatively more freedom for the so-called "fellow travelers." (For details see Gleb Struve, *Russian Literature under Lenin and Stalin, 1917–1953* (Norman: University of Oklahoma Press, 1971).

CHAPTER THREE

Time and Eternity

"Ты—вечности заложник
У времени в плену!"

(*Сочинения*, III, 82)

"*You are a hostage of eternity
Kept prisoner by time.*"

NOT UNEXPECTEDLY, the principal form that history assumes in Pasternak's work is that of the Revolution. The relationship of poetry and history—referring mainly to contemporary social and political events—occupies a prominent place in Pasternak's work beginning with the 1920's. In "Lofty Malady" (1923, 1928) the role of poetry is assessed against the epic proportions of the Revolution. In the poems of the early 1930's Pasternak repeatedly returns to the poet's paradoxical position in a socialist state. He attempts to accept the existing regime and searches for its justification.

Pasternak's views on the role of an individual in history and on the conflict between a creative individual and society are reflected in both "Lofty Malady" and "Lieutenant Schmidt" (1926–1927). An artist's alienation from society becomes very pronounced in the novel in verse *Spektorsky* (1925–1930). "Society" in Pasternak disregards the absolute value of an individual; it attempts to deprive him of his innate right to freedom.

Pasternak's insistence on the freedom of an individual does not mean, however, that his creative individual exists in separation from other people. In fact, the immortality of a poet depends on the creative response of his readers. What underlies the problem of the poet's relationship to society, as reflected in Pasternak's work, is essentially the conflict between the eternal and the temporal. Pasternak rejected the opposition of the creative artist and an average man, the opposition that was fundamental for the romantic and the symbolist world view. By defending his own freedom, the poet implicitly defends the freedom of every individual. Pasternak's poet cannot be in agreement with a society that negates the reality of the spiritual principle in man.

In *Doctor Zhivago* the ultimate purpose of history is spoken of as the overcoming of death; and it is not surprising that the "dead history" of the Soviet state—which subordinates reality to an idea—is rejected as a betrayal of life. It is in the name of life—which for Pasternak by definition is immortal—that he comes to reject temporal ideologies and systems.

THE POET AND HISTORY

When experienced directly, historical events often are meaningless and unpleasant, because it takes time to discern the true meaning of facts, to concoct a "sauce" that will make the "pie" more palatable:

Чреду веков питает новость,
Но золотой ее пирог,
Пока преданье варит соус,
Встает нам горла поперек.

The course of centuries is nourished by novelty,
But its golden pie—
While tradition is preparing a sauce—
Gets stuck in our throats.

As an illustration of this, Pasternak gives his impressions of a meeting that he attended at the Ninth Congress of the Soviets. The passing of time mercifully obliterates petty details:

Теперь из некоторой дали
Не видишь пошлых мелочей,
Забылся трафарет речей,
И время сгладило детали,
А мелочи преобладали.[1]

[1] *Sočinenija*, I, 269.

Now, from a certain distance,
One does not see the banal details.
The commonplace quality of the speeches has been forgotten.
Time erased the fine points,
And yet the details predominated.

In the introduction to *Spektorsky*, Pasternak implores poetry not to abandon sweeping breadth for the sake of details. Poetry should strive to preserve the "live precision," which is much more than the details:

Поэзия, не поступайся ширью.
Храни живую точность: точность тайн.
Не занимайся точками в пунктире
И зерен в мере хлеба не считай.[2]

Poetry, do not relinquish breadth.
Preserve the live precision: precision of mysteries.
Do not occupy yourself with the dots in a dotted line,
Do not count kernels in a measure of grain.

There is, however, a danger of losing this "live precision" with the passing of time. Together with the insignificant details, the essential characteristics of the events may be carried away. Setting out to depict the events of the 1905 revolution in "Девятьсот пятый год" ("The Year 1905," 1925–1926), the poet points out the necessity of speaking about the events while they still are alive for those who experienced them:

Это было при нас. / Это с нами вошло в поговорку,
И уйдет. / И однако, / За быстрою сменою лет,
Стерся след, / Словно год / Стал нулем меж девятки
   с пятеркой.
Стерся след, / Были нет, / От нее не осталось примет.[3]

It happened in our time. / It became proverbial with us,
And it will pass. / And despite this, / With the quick change
   of years,

[2] *Sočinenija*, I, 307.
[3] *Ibid.*, I, 110.

The trace has been erased, / As if the year / Became the zero between the nine and the five.

The trace has been erased, / The certainty of facts is no more, / There are no signs of it left.

Over the years Pasternak patiently searched for the true meaning of historical events witnessed by his generation; he succeeded in attaining that perspective—of which he already speaks in the works of the late twenties—only in his novel, *Doctor Zhivago*.

This was no mean accomplishment on Pasternak's part, because, for the members of his generation, it was not only the natural causes—the passage of time and the importance of the succeeding historical developments—that caused the memory of the earlier events to fade fast. Much more effective in the eradication of memory was a steadily growing official tendency to reinterpret historical facts or to "eliminate" them altogether. This feature of the Soviet approach to history—utterly degrading to human dignity and intelligence—is brilliantly analyzed by the widow of the poet Osip Mandelstam. In her first book of reminiscences, Nadezhda Mandelstam speaks of the majority of the potential witnesses to their time—the intellectuals of hers and Pasternak's generation—as people who (if they were lucky enough to outlive Stalin), with age and under pressure of official reinterpretation, lost not only the memory of the events, but the true understanding of the times and their own point of view, and so could not any longer qualify as witnesses.[4]

In "Lofty Malady" Pasternak returns to the problem with which he was concerned in his 1916 article "Black Goblet": the relationship of poetry to history, that is, to the political and social aspects of life. Pasternak wrote that life is gravitating toward two opposing poles: poetry and history. Equal value was assigned to each, but the poet insisted on not crossing the

---

[4] Nadežda Mandel'štam, *Vospominanija* (New York: Chekhov Publishing House, 1970), p. 319. English translation by Max Hayward, *Hope Against Hope* (New York: Atheneum, 1970).

border from one to the other. Pasternak's long poems of the twenties can be viewed as an attempt to bring together poetry and history, to cross the boundary between the two. The conclusions to which Pasternak came in *Doctor Zhivago* show that in the end he did not follow the path suggested by the critics and traveled by many of his contemporaries.

In the opening stanzas of "Lofty Malady," the value of history and poetry no longer appears equal. The magnitude of the events of the Revolution dwarfs poetry. It becomes merely the "lofty malady" of the title. Under the catastrophic circumstances poetry cannot be accepted as a normal condition; it is an abnormality. The poet is even ashamed of his gift of song:

> Мне стыдно и день ото дня стыдней,
> Что в век таких теней
> Высокая одна болезнь
> Еще зовется песнь.

> I become more ashamed with every passing day,
> That in the age of such shadows
> A certain lofty malady
> Is still called song.

But what disturbs him even more is using poetry for proclaiming that which is only imagined as the really existing, for taking well-meaning intentions as actual facts:

> Благими намереньями вымощен ад.
> Установился взгляд,
> Что, если вымостить ими стихи,
> Простятся все грехи.[5]

> Hell is paved with good intentions.
> There is an accepted view
> That if one paves his poems with them,
> All sins will be forgiven.

The poet is highly critical of the trend that encourages a poetry that is rooted in the realm of the desirable rather than of the

---

[5] *Sočinenija*, I, 264.

existing. Pasternak discusses the same subject in an article written in response to the 1925 party resolution on literature. He admits that he was often tempted to believe that "dreams can replace facts" and that coherently formulated aims necessarily reflect the actual state of affairs.[6]

The picture of the Revolution in "Lofty Malady" is contradictory: it is perceived both as an approaching spring and as a threat of future privations. Even at the time when the appearances of the old order were still preserved, the approach of the years of famine and destruction was unmistakable:

И по водопроводной сети
Взбирался кверху тот пустой,
Сосущий клекот лихолетья.[7]

And along the water pipes
Crawled up that empty,
Sucking screech of the years of disaster.

Pasternak's retrospective picture is akin to Blok's forebodings of the approaching destruction of traditions and culture in general, which he described in 1906 as "the time of the doors thrust open onto the square, the hearths extinguished, the windows darkened."[8] In a passage eliminated from the later editions, Pasternak depicted the Revolution as a raging blizzard. At first Pasternak's blizzard does not realize its own power and expects resistance from the world into which it is about to intrude. Soon the surprising discovery is made that there is no resistance because the houses are no longer inhabited:

Но скоро открывает иней,
Что нет под крылышками стрех
Ни вьюшек, ни души в помине,
И снегу жаловаться грех.[9]

---

[6] *Ibid.*, ш, 157.
[7] *Ibid.*, ı, 266.
[8] Aleksandr Blok, *Sobranie sočinenij v vos'mi tomax* (Moskva-Leningrad: GIXL, 1960), v, 71.
[9] *Sočinenija*, ı, 396.

But soon the hoarfrost discovers
That there are neither dampers under the eaves of the roof,
Nor a soul in the house,
And the snow has no reason to complain.

"Ни души в помине"—"not a soul" followed by "not a trace"—is quite emphatic. Coming after "ни вьюшек"—"no dampers"—which effectively keep the heat of a furnace from escaping, the line creates a picture of the lack of physical warmth as well as of spiritual essence. The external forces, represented by the blizzard, find no resistance in entering the house. The passage ends with another reminiscence of Blok (the line kept in the later editions): "Звук исчез / За гулом выросших небес"[10] ("Sound disappeared / In the rumble of the expanded heavens"). Pasternak's revolution in "Lofty Malady," like Blok's, is an elemental force destroying the old world and its way of life. The drowning of the sound by the noise of the events emphasizes the negative, destructive aspects of the upheaval.

Musing upon the revolutionary events, the poet is suddenly abandoned by the feeling of shame for his "lofty malady" and experiences an acute realization of the necessity of being faithful to one's principles:

Здесь места нет стыду.
Нельзя три раза, егозя,
Смотреть по-разному в глаза.

There is no place for shame here.
One cannot look straight into the eyes
Three times in a different fashion, fidgeting and shifting.

Here Pasternak turns to the problem that proved to be crucial for the later development of literature in the Soviet Union and his own position in it. No matter what their magnitude and import, historical events cannot detract from the absolute value of such qualities as honesty or faithfulness to one's beliefs. The ambiguity of poetry seems insignificant alongside the prevalent

[10] *Ibid.*, I, 266.

mentality that labels people "enemies": "Еще двусмысленней, / чем песнь, / Тупое слово 'враг'"[11] ("Even more ambiguous than song, / Is the blunt word 'enemy'"). It is not the question of being for or against a particular cause, but the attitude of hatred to which the poet objects.

What was contradictory in "Lofty Malady" became clearly polarized in *Doctor Zhivago*. The unconditional and joyful acceptance of the Revolution in 1917 remained. Zhivago thinks of the Revolution on a cosmic scale and senses greatness in its directness and its disregard for everything that stands in its way. Later, having attained a certain perspective, he clearly distinguishes between the Revolution itself and the regime that issued from it. He still thinks of the summer of 1917 as the time when the Revolution was "a god descended from heaven to earth." Pasternak notes that Zhivago's lament over his loss of Lara in his Varykino poems was partly a lament over the loss of the Revolution as it appeared to him in 1917. Finally, Zhivago comes to a conclusion that the fate of revolutions is invariably self-defeat. They are short-lived, and what remains when they pass is a fanatical devotion to the narrowmindedness of their leaders.[12] The bitter truth is that revolution is used as a banner long after its actual disappearance.

In "Lieutenant Schmidt" the state appears as an idol that forever lingers on the threshold of freedom: ("О государства истукан, / Свободы вечное преддверье!"[13] ("O, idol of the state, / [You are] An eternal threshold of freedom!"). A revolution that destroys the existing oppressive state leads to suppression again. Pasternak compares this to the inevitable step from Christian martyrdom in the arenas of Rome to the regimentation of the Roman Church: "И вечно делается шаг / От римских цирков к римской церкви" ("And over and over the step is made / From Roman circuses to the Roman Church"). The October Revolution did not alter this

[11] *Ibid.*, I, 267.

[12] *Ibid.*, IV, 466. The transitory nature of revolutions is also stressed in Gromeko's recollections of the events of 1917 (*Sočinenija*, IV, 247).

[13] *Ibid.*, I, 145.

85

sequence: "И мы живем по той же мерке, / Мы, люди катакомб и шахт"[14] ("And we live according to that very standard, / We, the people of the catacombs and mines"). Although not stated as emphatically and categorically as in *Doctor Zhivago*, the indictment of the regime that followed the Revolution is quite clear. By placing the Roman Church side by side with "the idol of the state" and by indicating that the development remains unaltered in our time, Pasternak considers any religious, social, or political utopia doomed to failure.

It has to be emphasized, however, that Zhivago accepts the social and economic changes brought about by the Revolution. He admits that in the life style of his class before the Revolution there were too many superfluous elements, the elimination of which he approves.[15] Pasternak considered the new attitude toward accumulation of wealth and property as a positive achievement of the Revolution in Russia. References to this point abound in the accounts of Pasternak's conversations with his Western visitors during the last few years of his life.[16]

Soon after the Revolution, Zhivago realizes that the cultural elite, of which he is a part, is doomed to destruction, but he accepts this also.[17] This realization Pasternak voiced long before in "Lofty Malady":

Мы были музыкой во льду.
Я говорю про всю среду,
С которой я имел в виду
Сойти со сцены, и сойду.[18]

We were music in ice.
I have in mind my whole circle,
With which I intended to
And shall leave the stage.

[14] *Ibid.*, I, 146.

[15] *Ibid.*, IV, 173.

[16] See Ruge, *op.cit.*, pp. 22–25, and Hélène Peltier-Zamoyska, "Pasternak, homme du passé?" *op.cit.*, pp. 16–29.

[17] *Sočinenija*, IV, 187.

[18] *Ibid.*, I, 267.

The poet searches for a justification of this situation. Yury Zhivago thinks he finds it in the imaginary good that the Revolution brought to the people. On his way to the Urals, he rejoices at the "normal" life of the countryside that he observes from the train. He wants to believe that the peasants have profited from the new system. Unfortunately, this is only an illusion, as the down-to-earth realist Kostoed-Amursky, who travels on the same train, does not fail to inform Zhivago.[19]

"Другу" ("To a Friend"), a poem written in 1931, is built on the same assumption that the regime is good for the majority of the people and bad only for a few like the poet himself:

> Иль я не знаю, что, в потемки тычась,
> Во век не вышла б к свету темнота,
> И я—урод, и счастье сотен тысяч
> Не ближе мне пустого счастья ста?

> As if I do not know that groping in the dark,
> Ignorance would never find light,
> Or am I a monster, and the happiness of the hundreds of thousands
> Is not dearer to me than the empty happiness of a hundred?

This poem has often been quoted in connection with Pasternak's unsuccessful attempts to reconcile poetry with socialism. The poet acknowledges a rational desire and makes an honest effort to accept the socialist reality: "И разве я не мерюсь пятилеткой, / Не падаю, не подымаюсь с ней?" ("Don't I use the five-year plan as a standard, / Don't I fall and rise with it?"). This, however, does not help to solve the problem, because he cannot renounce his calling, which is an inherent part of his being: "Но как мне быть с моей грудною клеткой / И с тем, что всякой косности косней?" ("But what am I to do with my rib cage, / And with that which is more inert than inertia itself?"). Here Pasternak comes to a realization that the building of socialism and the calling of a poet are mutually exclusive.

[19] *Ibid.*, IV, 228.

The poem "To a Friend" was usually considered by Soviet critics as Pasternak's admission of guilt: his inability to break with the irrational and the intuitive while acknowledging that socialism constitutes a triumph of reason.[20] Giving socialism its due, Pasternak frankly admits that poets might be dangerou⌐ for the state:

Напрасно в дни великого совета,
Где высшей страсти отданы места,
Оставлена вакансия поэта:
Она опасна, если не пуста.[21]

It is unfortunate that at the time of the great [historical] decisions,
When preference is given to a higher passion,
The post of a poet is retained:
It is dangerous, if not vacant.

This stanza is rather ambiguous and allows for different interpretations. The final qualifying statement, *если не пуста*, can be interpreted either as the possibility of the poet's position remaining vacant or being physically occupied, but remaining meaningless and insignificant. The former interpretation was dismissed by at least one critic as an impossibility in Soviet times.[22] Pasternak's warning that a poet's position can be dangerous should be addressed, in the critic's opinion, solely to the author of the poem.

But the poem "To a Friend" says not only that. The danger of which Pasternak speaks in the poem refers primarily to the state and only as a consequence to the poet. The poet accepts the conclusions drawn in *The Republic* of Plato: since the power of a poet is great, it has to be controlled and utilized for the good of the state.

[20] See, for instance, R. Miller-Budnickaja, "O 'filosofii iskusstva' B. Pasternaka i R. M. Ril'ke," *Zvezda*, No. 5 (1932), pp. 160–68.

[21] *Sočinenija*, I, 223.

[22] A. Selivanovskij, "Poèzija opasna?" *Literaturnaja Gazeta*, August 15, 1931.

Pasternak regrets retaining the "post" of poet at a time when social and political concerns have, presumably, an undisputed priority. In a socialist state, as in Plato's ideal state, there is no place for uncontrolled art that inevitably becomes dangerous for the state itself. The poet foresees the unavoidable conflict between the purpose of the ideocratic state and art, which places upon the artist demands of its own.

Beginning with the time of the first five-year plan, literature was expected to make a tangible contribution to the building of socialism. Although Pasternak's selected poems and his long poems about the 1905 Revolution were republished several times before 1936, no other original books of his appeared between 1932 and 1943. It was not until the time of the publication of *Doctor Zhivago* in the West that the truth of Pasternak's supposition was most vividly illustrated: the fear of those in power and, as a result, the sad consequences for the poet.

In the poems of *Второе рождение* (*Second Birth*, 1932), Pasternak's feelings toward the building of socialism in Russia are as contradictory as the juxtaposition of the near and the far in the line "Ты рядом, даль социализма" ("You are at hand, distant expanse of socialism"). Theoretically Pasternak accepts socialism, but the Soviet reality is not socialism; the ideal state has not been realized: "Ты куришься сквозь дым теорий, / Страна вне сплетен и клевет" ("You are barely visible through the smoke of theories, / The country beyond gossip and slander"). Now the poet finds a justification of the existing system in the admittedly improved life of women in the Soviet Union: "Ты край, где женщины в Путивле / Зегзицами не плачут впредь"[23] ("You are the land where women / Henceforth no longer cry like cuckoo birds in Putivl"). The reference here is to Prince Igor's wife, lamenting her husband's captivity in *The Tale of Igor's Campaign*. Her anguish probably represents the suffering of women in general, but it is not clear what "improvements" could alleviate the situation alluded to in those lines. The poem ends on a very

---

[23] *Sočinenija*, I, 326.

optimistic note of faith in the happiness of the future generations:

> Где голос, посланный вдогонку
> Необоримой новизне,
> Весельем моего ребенка
> Из будущего вторит мне.[24]

> Where the voice sent after
> Invincible novelty
> Echoes from the future
> With the joy of my child.

In another poem of the same book, the beneficial changes in women's lot become the reason for the poet's acceptance of the demands made by the regime on the individual:

> И так как с малых детских лет
> Я ранен женской долей,
> И след поэта—только след
> Ее путей, не боле,
> И так как я лишь ей задет
> И ей у нас раздолье,
> То весь я рад сойти на-нет
> В революцьонной воле[25]

> And because from my early childhood
> [My sensibility] has been wounded by women's lot,
> And the poet's trace is only a trace
> Of her paths, no more,
> And because I am touched only by her,
> And she is free to do as she likes in our country,
> I am ready to vanish entirely
> In the revolutionary will.

The theme of the improvement of women's fate is not confined to those two poems. Although not connected with the

---

[24] *Ibid.*, I, 327.
[25] *Ibid.*, I, 360.

Revolution, it is the primary concern of both the protagonist of *A Tale* and the poet-improvisator in the story that the protagonist writes. It is also an important theme in *Doctor Zhivago*. The pre-revolutionary system and way of life are renounced in the name of the wronged woman. In his last conversation with Zhivago, Antipov-Strelnikov speaks of the Revolution as a revenge for the misfortunes and contradictions of Lara's life. Sima Tuntseva mentions the rights of women as the self-evident achievement of the Revolution.[26]

In "Весенний день тридцатого апреля" ("A Spring Day of the Thirtieth of April"), a poem written on the occasion of the May Day celebration in 1931, the development and strengthening of the positive qualities in Soviet life are seen simply as a matter of time:

Но с каждой годовщиной все махровей
Тугой задаток розы будет цвесть,
Всё явственнее прибывать здоровье,
И всё заметней искренность и честь.

But with every anniversary more luxuriantly
Will bloom the tight bud of a rose,
More noticeably will increase the health,
More prominent will be sincerity and honor.

The general impression this poem leaves is that of unfounded optimism; Pasternak ends it on a hint of some spiritual transformation that will result from the passing of time:

Пока, как запах мокрых центифолий,
Не вырвется, не выразится вслух,
Не сможет не сказаться поневоле
Созревших лет перебродивший дух.[27]

Until, like the fragrance of wet roses,
The fermented spirit of the matured years
Will not break out, will not express itself audibly,
Will not be able not to show itself as the inevitable result.

[26] *Ibid.*, iv, 472–73, 423.
[27] *Ibid.*, i, 358.

In "Столетье с лишним—не вчера" ("More than a century —it was not yesterday"), a variation on Pushkin's "В надежде славы и добра" ("Hoping for the glory and for the good"), the poet, although aware of the facts, succumbs to the temptation of hope against hope:

Столетье с лишним—не вчера,
А сила прежняя в соблазне
В надежде славы и добра
Глядеть на вещи без боязни.

More than a century—it was not yesterday—
But there is the same power in the temptation,
Hoping for the glory and for the good,
To look at things without fear.

Trying to find consolation in a historical parallel, Pasternak uses Pushkin's comparison of the contemporary situation (in Pushkin's case, the crushing of the Decembrist revolt by Nicholas I) to that of the beginning of Peter the Great's reign. Although the poet speaks about hope, he knows very well that Pushkin's hope proved to be futile—Nicholas' reign did not get more liberal with time—and the implicit misgivings about the regime are only too evident.

Theoretical acceptance of the Revolution and its consequences and a vaguely utopian optimism, combined with a desperate search for a justification of the system in terms of real life, do not succeed in suppressing the pessimistic undercurrent present in those poems. The poet wishes to become one with the people and the system, to break away from his solitary confinement: "Хотеть ... / ... / Труда со всеми сообща / И заодно с правопорядком"[28] ("Wishing ... / ... / To work together with other people / And with the established order"). But contemporary life is permeated with falsity and intellectual sloth. The new regime has not changed people for the better. The poet is worn out by empty words, he seeks salvation in contact with life itself:

[28] *Ibid.*, I, 360.

Когда я устаю от пустозвонства
Во все века вертевшихся льстецов,
Мне хочется, как сон при свете солнца,
Припомнить жизнь и ей взглянуть в лицо.[29]

When I weary of the empty talk
Of the flatterers who dodge about in every age,
I wish to recollect life—like a dream recollected in sunlight—
And to look it in the face.

In search for a resolution of the incongruity between the theory
and practice of the system, the poet turns to the future:

Когда ж от смерти не спасет таблетка,
То тем свободней время поспешит
В ту даль, куда вторая пятилетка
Протягивает тезисы души.[30]

But when a pill will not prevent death,
Then will time rush forward even more freely
Toward that faraway distance into which the second five-year
    plan
Is extending the theses of the soul.

There are some obvious contradictions in Pasternak's
attitude toward the socialist state. His consistent emphasis on
the future relegates socialism to the realm of the unattainable
even in the poems of *Second Birth*.

It is not hard to agree with Gleb Struve that Pasternak was
"never quite at home in Soviet literature";[31] but he cannot be
considered a complete stranger in it, either from the official or
from the poet's own point of view. Bukharin's highly positive
appraisal of Pasternak's poetry in his programmatic speech at
the Congress of the Union of Soviet Writers in 1934 is sufficient proof of the official position at that time.[32] The period

[29] *Ibid.*, I, 351.
[30] *Ibid.*, I, 352.
[31] Gleb Struve, *Russian Literature under Lenin and Stalin*, p. 181.
[32] N. Buxarin, *Poèzija, poètika i zadači poètičeskogo tvorčestva v SSSR*
(GIXL, 1934), pp. 53–56.

from the late 1920's through 1936 has to be considered as a time when the poet very conscientiously tried to adjust to the official line.

A very perceptive analysis of the reasons why Pasternak's open break with the official line in Soviet literature came only at the end of his life with the publication of *Doctor Zhivago* is made by Nadezhda Mandelstam in her *Reminiscences.* She observes that Pasternak's conscious efforts to find common ground with contemporary Soviet literature were facilitated by his having some points of contact with traditional literature and, above all, by being a Muscovite and therefore, in a sense, "belonging" to Soviet literature.[33] Pasternak's own assessment of his place in contemporary Soviet literature and his position vis-à-vis his time will be discussed in detail in a later section of this chapter.

IDEOLOGY AND LIFE

Over the years Pasternak moves from a personal, intuitive rejection of socialism in the form practiced in the Soviet Union to a more rational and generalized rejection of the very tenets of the Soviet regime. If in the poem "To a Friend" socialism was considered beneficial for the people and the poet's inability to accept it was explained as an anomaly peculiar to him as a poet, in *Doctor Zhivago* Pasternak acknowledges the system's general corrupting influence on individuals. A desire to come face to face with life without the intermediary of ideologies or theoretical programs becomes more pronounced. Pasternak's rejection of the regime is essentially of an existential nature. It is a free human personality that he defends against an ideology. His revolt is in the name of life itself. Zhivago at one point explains the change in his attitude toward the Revolution in vaguely Tolstoyan terms: "I used to be very revolutionary, but now I think that nothing can be gained by brute force. People must be drawn to good by goodness."[34]

[33] Nadežda Mandel'štam, *op.cit.*, pp. 158–59, 164.
[34] *Sočinenija*, IV, 270 (Hayward-Harari, p. 261).

The editorial board of *Новый Мир* accused Pasternak and the protagonist of his novel of changing their views of the Revolution because of personal inconveniences and disappointments.[35] The accusation is not to the point in either case. Upon his return to Moscow, Zhivago renounces all material comfort and any semblance of normal life so as not to be forced to compromise his principles. Zhivago repeatedly affirms an individual's right to freedom, a right to shape his own life. At one point he approaches Dostoevsky's underground man in his defiance of logic that disregards human freedom: "I'll say 'A' but I won't say 'B'—no matter what you do."[36]

In the summer of 1917, upon his return from the front, Zhivago is appalled at the change that his friends have undergone since their last meeting. The loss of original thought and opinion has made them all uniformly colorless and common. Later in the novel, Lara sees the source of all falsity and evil in Russian life in the loss of faith in the individual, in the fear of being different from others, and in the inability to defend one's own point of view.[37]

Pasternak's repeated attempts to assert the rights of the individual stem not from a desire for individualistic separation from other people, but from a necessity of reminding his contemporaries of the worth of an individual. It is in this light that Pasternak's negative evaluation of his own participation in the pre-revolutionary futurist group Centrifuge should be viewed. In *Safe Conduct* he characterized the period of his participation in Centrifuge as the time when he was "playing at group discipline" and constantly sacrificing both his taste and conscience to it.[38] This negative attitude toward organized groups and their influence on an individual is reiterated in more general terms in the novel. Zhivago's uncle speaks of the early years of the century as a period when everyone strived to

[35] *Novyj Mir*, No. 11 (1958), pp. iii–xvi.
[36] *Sočinenija*, IV, 348.
[37] *Ibid.*, IV, 177, 414.
[38] *Ibid.*, II, 269.

belong to a group. For him, however, this reveals the herd instinct of man and a lack of individual talent.[39] To follow his own individual way in life was of primary importance for Pasternak. Standing alone, having his own opinion, became one of the most characteristic traits of Pasternak's life in a totalitarian society that demanded from an individual continuous participation in various group actions.

A typical example of Pasternak's efforts to preserve his individuality within the workings of the Soviet system is his adding of a postscript to his fellow writers' letter of condolence to Stalin on the death of Nadezhda Allilueva. He wrote that he shared the feelings of his colleagues and added that on the night of Nadezhda Allilueva's death he—for the first time, as a poet—was persistently thinking of Stalin. The coincidence made him feel that he almost witnessed her death. The effects of this postscript on the poet's fortunes have been judged by several commentators as highly beneficial; even his survival during the purges has been ascribed to the influence of this personal note.[40]

Pasternak's attempts to act as an individual were not lost on his more orthodox colleagues. He was accused of placing himself apart from others, and of "pretending" to have opinions different from the accepted ones. On one occasion, Pasternak's critic objected to his use of the verb "to yell" (*орать*), addressed to his opponents at a public discussion; the critic missed entirely the essence of the poet's plea against conformity: not to yell in unison.[41]

Ideology that becomes an object of deification and an aim in

---

[39] *Ibid.*, IV, 9.

[40] See Mixail Korjakov, "Termometr Rossii," *Novyj Žurnal*, 55 (1958), pp. 139–41, and Robert Conquest, *The Pasternak Affair: Courage of Genius* (Philadelphia and New York: J. B. Lippincott, 1962), p. 22. The letter and Pasternak's postscript appeared in *Literaturnaja Gazeta*, November 17, 1932.

[41] Aleksandr Fadeev, "Za podlinnuju demokratiju," *Literaturnaja Gazeta*, March 10, 1937, and Ja. Èjdel'man, *Literaturnaja Gazeta*, March 15, 1936. For a survey of official attacks on Pasternak, see Struve, *Russian Literature under Lenin and Stalin*.

itself invariably turns against life. In *Doctor Zhivago* people are shown to lose human qualities under the influence of ideology. Lara sees Antipov's face replaced by the embodiment of an idea. Antipov gives the impression of being bewitched (*казался заколдованным, как в сказке*) to his fellow officer Galliulin. Even more drastic is the change in the old revolutionaries Tiverzin and Antipov-senior. They are spoken of as lifeless idols devoid of human feelings.[42]

The dehumanizing effect is not limited to those who accept and serve the ideology; it also reaches those who are most remote from politics and power. Pasternak illustrates this point through the development of the two teenagers, Vasya Brykin and Terenty Galuzin, whose role in the novel is otherwise unessential. Although Galuzin first appears in the novel as a corrupted, degenerate, and extremely unpleasant youth just expelled from school, at this point he is guilty mostly of associating with dubious characters. Eventually he points out Strelnikov's hiding place to the authorities and thus becomes an instrument of his death.[43] Brykin, who, in contrast to Galuzin, is introduced as "unusually innocent and uncorrupted,"[44] in the end betrays Zhivago. Brykin's betrayal, however, is different from Galuzin's. In Brykin's case the attraction to simplistic slogans causes him to abandon his friend. Pasternak leaves no doubt in the reader's mind that this essentially good but simpleminded young man is able to achieve more in life thanks to the Revolution. But, as he is more and more captivated by the obviousness and primitivism of the "truths proclaimed by the Revolution," he begins to criticize and finally condemns Zhivago for his complexity and passivity, which seem to stand in the way of the new way of life.[45] An element of moral degradation is present in the actions of both Galuzin and Brykin, and the line of their moral development within the novel is unmistakably that of decline.

[42] *Sočinenija*, IV, 412, 116–17, 327.

[43] *Ibid.*, IV, 332–37, 470.

[44] *Ibid.*, IV, 227.

[45] *Ibid.*, IV, 487.

According to Zhivago, the failure of the regime originates in its attempts to change and to reform life by means of an ideology that has nothing to do with real life. Zhivago stresses that he objects to a generally utopian approach of "building life anew," because for him life is an ever-rejuvenating and dynamic principle rather than an inert material that can be shaped and molded to fit some abstract scheme.[46]

The protagonist of the novel could not better express the views of the author. If in 1916 Pasternak allotted equal importance to poetry and history and during the twenties and thirties was attempting to place the active reconstruction of life ahead of poetry, toward the end of his life he came to reject that "history" which is guided by "dead ideology." The distinction that Pasternak makes between this history and the one that is in contact with reality is very significant. In *Safe Conduct* he insisted that poetry "takes place in history and in collaboration with real life."[47] Although Pasternak does not see a poet involved in "making history," as a politician or a social leader might be, he places him in close contact with reality. Poetry, by being connected with life, is more significant than history, which deals with abstract programs.

Zhivago's definition of history is remarkably close to one of Pasternak's definitions of poetry that emphasizes its connections with life. In 1935, at the International Congress of Writers for the Defense of Culture in Paris, Pasternak spoke of poetry as being on the ground under our feet and in the grass over which we walk.[48] Zhivago compares history to the life of the vegetable kingdom. Like a forest whose growth is both imperceptible and striking, historical process is subject to organic development not controlled by individuals.[49] At the basis of these two definitions of poetry and history is their existential relevance: both have value only if connected with the actuality of life.

[46] *Ibid.*, IV, 268, 347–48.
[47] *Ibid.*, II, 277.
[48] "Slovo o poèzii," in *Sbornik statej, posvjaščennyx...*, p. 9.
[49] *Sočinenija*, IV, 465.

Zhivago is aware of a connection between his view and Tolstoy's idea of history as an organic process that individuals cannot change. But there are some important differences that should not be overlooked. Whereas Tolstoy's approach is invariably critical and analytical, Pasternak's is its opposite: affirmative and constructive. In line with this, unlike Tolstoy, Pasternak's poet is not interested in the analysis of the historical process itself, but is more concerned with the effects historical events have on individual people.[50]

Pasternak does not deprive individual leaders of all their power and significance as does Tolstoy. Zhivago compares their function to that of a ferment,[51] but, in keeping with Tolstoy's views, he relegates the actual "making of history" to the "insignificant" people whose names are not known. In "Смелость" ("Courage"), a poem from 1941, the numerous nameless defenders of the cities besieged by the Germans are directly concerned with events of great historical magnitude and significance: "Вы векам в глаза смотрели / С пригородных баррикад"[52] ("You looked centuries into the eyes / From the suburban barricades"). This view is essentially identical to the one expounded by Pasternak in "Black Goblet" (1916): on the battlefields of World War I, the soldiers met face to face with history.[53]

The problem of the role of the individual in history is

---

[50] Pasternak's interest in "problems of history" was not by choice as was Tolstoj's, but was forced on him by the contemporary historical events themselves and by the party policy in literature. His deep respect for Tolstoj did not prevent him, however, from arguing with Tolstoj on certain points in *Doktor Živago*. Živago's conscious preference for Puškin's and Čexov's modest unconcern with ultimate questions implies that an artist should be able to find answers to the questions that he is faced with in life *through his art* (*Sočinenija*, IV, 294–95). Another important disagreement with Tolstoj is on the relationship of the good and the beautiful. In a conversation with a Tolstoyan, Živago's uncle, Vedenjapin, speaks of the "beauty of truth" as a more important factor in the spiritual development of mankind than "moral teaching" (*Sočinenija*, IV, 42).

[51] *Sočinenija*, IV, 465–66.

[52] *Ibid.*, III, 35.

[53] *Ibid.*, III, 151.

touched upon in "Lofty Malady." Originally the poem ended in a passage depicting the historical moment of the abdication of Nicholas the Second. The Emperor himself did not appear in the poem; the events obviously were not controlled by him:

И уставал орел двуглавый,
По Псковской области кружа,
От стягивавшейся облавы
Неведомого мятежа.

....

Сужался круг, редели сосны,
Два солнца встретились в окне.
Одно всходило из-за Тосна,
Другое заходило в Дне.[54]

The double-headed eagle was getting weary,
Circling about Pskov province,
[Dodging] the mysterious rebellion's
Tightening trap.

....

The circle was getting smaller, the pine trees were
    thinning out
Two suns met in the window.
One was rising from beyond Tosno,
The other was going down in Dno.

The significance of the historical events—the Emperor's abdication on a train car near Pskov and the revolution in Petrograd—are depicted without the appearance of the individuals responsible for the events. In the 1928 version of the work, Pasternak added a passage describing his impressions of Lenin's speech at the Ninth Congress of the Soviets. Although not clearly developed here, the juxtaposition of the two contrasting personalities points to the question of the role of the individual in history.

[54] *Ibid.*, I, 270–71.

100

In Pasternak's unpublished autobiographical notes Lenin appears as an exceptional personality, a genius, and a superman who accepts the responsibility for the destruction and human sacrifices that his actions and decisions have caused. By his own decision and will he sanctioned the Revolution with all its consequences: "He allowed the sea to get violent; the hurricane lashed out with his blessing."[55]

There is a certain similarity in Pasternak's approach to the role of Lenin and that of Lieutenant Schmidt. Although one is successful and the other fails, both are seen as creative individuals responsible for the consequences of the events that they set in motion.

Pasternak obviously admired Lenin's ability to assume power; eventually, however, he did question Lenin's right to do so. The 1965 *Библиотека поэта* version of "Lofty Malady" ends on a note of doubt about Lenin's role:

Тогда его увидев въяве,
Я думал, думал без конца
Об авторстве его и праве
Дерзать от первого лица.
Из ряда многих поколений
Выходит кто-нибудь вперед.
Предвестьем льгот приходит гений
И гнетом мстит за свой уход.[56]

Having actually seen him then,
I thought and thought without end
About his authorship and his right
To dare to act in the first person.
From a series of many generations
Someone steps forward.
A genius comes as a forerunner of privileges,
But takes revenge for his departure by oppression.

---

[55] Quoted in notes to "Vysokaja bolezn'," *Stixotvorenija*, p. 655. Unfortunately, the date of writing is not mentioned.

[56] *Ibid.*, p. 244.

By imposing his will upon the people, an outstanding leader deprives them of their freedom.[57]

Pasternak returned in his novel to the person of Nicholas the

[57] To leave out the few hints we have of Pasternak's opinion of Stalin and his role would be avoiding one of the very important problems of the time. Nadežda Mandel'štam speaks of Pasternak's almost pathological interest in the person of Stalin in 1934. This, certainly, was not unique; the general and all-pervasive adulation of Stalin was shared by many intellectuals. Stalin was considered the embodiment of the times, of history, and of the future. Nadežda Mandel'štam's source of information on Pasternak's attitude is Pasternak himself. During their conversation after Stalin's famous telephone call about Osip Mandel'štam (June 1934), Pasternak confided to her his great disappointment that he could not arrange for a personal meeting with Stalin. After this "failure" he could not write poetry for a long time. (Nadežda Mandel'štam, *Vospominanija*, p. 155).

Pasternak's postscript to the writers' letter of condolence to Stalin on the death of Nadežda Allilueva indicates that he had an interest in the person of Stalin at least as early as 1932. We can assume as an important contributing factor toward this interest the influence of Pasternak's discovery of Georgia, where he went for the first time in the summer of 1931. On many occasions afterwards he emphasized the importance of the "Georgian chapter" in his life and work. There were many reasons why Pasternak was so enthusiastic about Georgia and the Georgians—he describes them eloquently in his *Avtobiografičeskij očerk*. It is not unlikely that one of the areas in which Georgia played a role in Pasternak's life was his enhanced interest in Stalin.

Two poems of Pasternak's, both published in *Izvestija* on New Year's Day of 1936, are concerned with Stalin. The first poem, "Ja ponjal: vse živo" ("I realized: everything is alive"), dated 1935, expresses the poet's gratitude to the leaders and teachers of mankind. The realization that evokes the poet's gratitude is of the unity and the interdependence of our civilization. Lenin and Stalin and the poet's verses are seen as part of the same three-thousand-year process. (*Sočinenija*, III, 138).

The second poem, "Mne po duše stroptivyj norov" ("I like [his] obstinacy"), consists of two parts: in the first the poet's life and destiny are appraised; part two, in a parallel development, gives the view of Stalin's historical role; its subject is Stalin's extraordinary greatness:

A v te že dni na rasstojan'i,
Za drevnej kamennoj stenoj,
Živet ne čelovek—dejan'e,
Postupok rostom v šar zemnoj.

Second. Although he is struck by a frightening lack of any
manifestation of strong personality in the Emperor whom he
sees in Galicia, Zhivago praises his lack of artificiality and
theatricality.[58] Zhivago's sympathies are with the weak and
unsuccessful leader who is tragic in his simplicity and artless-
ness. In this preference for the unheroic and in the dismissal of
the patriotic speeches as theatrical and banal, there is a vague
but unmistakable similarity to Tolstoy's condemnation of
Napoleon in *War and Peace*. But Pasternak goes a step beyond
Tolstoy. Tolstoy deglamorizes both historical and fictional
"heroes." Pasternak omits them altogether. Antipov-Strelnikov—the only major character who has the temperamental
makings of a "hero"—is destroyed by the cause he serves: he
is forced into the spiritual dead end of suicide. There are no

During the very same days, at a distance,
Beyond the ancient, stone wall,
There lives not a man but a deed,
An action whose dimensions equal the globe.

The opposition of Stalin's superhuman achievements to his unchanging
humanity ("No on ostalsja čelovekom") is very much in the spirit of
the thirties. This poem verifies the truth of Nadežda Mandel'štam's
statement. The last two stanzas emphasize the poet's deep concern for
the "genius" and his belief that, despite his own insignificance, the
acknowledgment of the other's role is mutual:

Kak v ètoj dvuxgolosnoj fuge
On sam ni beskonečno mal,
On verit v znan'e drug o druge
Predel'no krajnix dvux načal.

(*Sočinenija*, III, 241)

No matter how infinitesimally small he himself is
In this two-voiced fugue,
He believes that the two opposing principles
Know about each other's existence.

Of these two poems only the first part of the second poem was included
in collections of Pasternak's verse. After the original publication, both
poems were reprinted a few months later in the journal *Znamja* together
with another five poems, three of which thematically are connected with
Georgia. (*Sočinenija*, III, 240–42; *Stixotvorenija*, p. 681).

[58] *Sočinenija*, IV, 123.

victories in the novel, and the characters are not inspired by patriotism not only because the times and events in *Doctor Zhivago* are different from those in *War and Peace*, but because these matters are not essential for Pasternak, as is clearly demonstrated in the person and in the views of the protagonist.

For Pasternak, the freedom of every individual is of primary importance, and therefore the right of leaders to deprive individuals of their freedom is questioned and eventually condemned. In *Doctor Zhivago* the leaders who accomplished the Revolution are no longer seen as outstanding creative individuals, but as "fanatical men of action with one-track minds."[59] The Nietzschean concept of the extraordinary individual with unlimited power and rights is superseded by a basically Christian conception that places more emphasis on the value and the rights of *every* individual rather than on those of the chosen few. In *Doctor Zhivago* the essence of Christianity is spoken of as the "mystery of personality" that places the individual above the society, the state, and the nation.[60]

[59] *Ibid.*, IV, 466.

[60] *Ibid.*, IV, 125. Pasternak's unquestionable acceptance of the economic aspects of socialism and his categorical rejection of its anti-humanistic tendencies are very close to the views of Berdjaev, who saw the source of the anti-personalistic character of communism in the Marxist assumption that an individual is only a function of social process, and does not possess any intrinsic value. This assumption leads to the inevitable subjugation of the individual to society. Berdjaev distinguishes between individual, as a social and biological category, and personality, as a spiritual category. As an individual, man is a part of society and of biological genus; as a personality, he is an integral, existential nucleus and as such has a right to freedom from society ("Personalizm i marksizm," *Put'*, 48 [1935], pp. 3–19).

Pasternak's acceptance of the economic aspects of socialism, however, does not prevent him from judging positively the cultural role of the Russian nineteenth-century bourgeoisie, as is indicated by the character of Proxor in the drafts of his play "Slepaja krasavica" (New York: Harcourt, Brace and World, Inc., 1969). See also the account of Olga Carlisle in "Three Visits with Boris Pasternak," *The Paris Review*, 24 (Summer-Fall 1960), pp. 45–69.

THE POET AND HIS TIME

The 1920's—the period when the problem of the relationship of poetry and history began to gain prominence in Pasternak's work, when he turned to the subject of the 1905 Revolution in "The Year 1905" and "Lieutenant Schmidt" and to the assessment of the poet's place in contemporary society in "Lofty Malady" and *Spektorsky*—were the time of his correspondence with Marina Tsvetaeva. Both poets had similar views of the relationship between a poet and his time, of the paradoxical phenomenon of the timelessness of art and its irrevocable connection with its time.

"Lofty Malady" (1923, 1928) and *Spektorsky* (1924–1930) demonstrate the poet's alienation from contemporary literature and society. It is not inconceivable that in addition to Pasternak's personal circumstances and the current developments in Soviet literature, his friendship and correspondence with Tsvetaeva were an influence in this respect. Tsvetaeva's was a much more direct and uncompromising rejection of "our time." She was acutely aware of not being recognized and appreciated by her contemporaries; for her this was consistent with the essence of "our time." Although the poet's conflict with his time is quite pronounced in Pasternak's works of the period, he is reluctant to accept this as inevitable. He is more optimistic than Tsvetaeva, and the rejection of the poet by his time—although undeniable—appears to him as an unfortunate mistake rather than the unavoidable development.

There is some circumstantial evidence that makes one believe that Marina Tsvetaeva's personality and her friendship with Pasternak were reflected in the character of Maria Ilyina and her relations with the protagonist of *Spektorsky*.[61] In the introduction to *Spektorsky*, the author speaks of the impressions he formed (on the basis of articles in foreign publications)

[61] The evidence is not presented here because it is the subject of a separate study examining the Pasternak-Cvetaeva friendship as it is reflected in *Spektorskij*, *Povest'*, and "Lejtenant Šmidt." See "Boris Pasternak i Marina Cvetaeva (K istorii družby)," *Vestnik R.S.X.D.* (Paris), 100 (1971), pp. 281–305.

105

about the work of a fictitious poetess Maria Ilyina. The role of "our time" in shaping the life of the poet is what he perceived most vividly in the accounts of her poetry:

Где, верно всё, что было слез и снов,
И до крови кроил наш век закройщик,
Простерлось красотой без катастроф
И стало правдой сроков без отсрочки.[62]

Where, I suppose, all tears and dreams—
And where our century the cutter cut [the fabric] so that
    blood would show—
Stretched out as beauty without catastrophes,
And became the truth of deadlines without delay.

"Our time" appears as an actively malevolent force in the dedication to "Lieutenant Schmidt," which is an acrostic reading "to Marina Tsvetaeva." "Our time" is pursuing its victim, the poet, through life, the way a hunter pursues a beast through a forest. The hunt continues through the centuries and the problem is only tentatively resolved; at least for the present, life seems to outbalance the cruel time. Pasternak addresses his time directly: "Век, отчего травить охоты нет?" ("O century, why do you have no desire to persecute?") and demands an answer both for himself and for Tsvetaeva: "Ответь листвой, стволами, сном ветвей / И ветром и травою мне и ей"[63] ("Respond through the leaves, the trunks, the sleepy branches, / Through wind and grass, respond to me and to her"). A beast can be concealed by the surrounding forest, the poet is surrounded by life that mollifies the demands of the age.

Dedicated to Tsvetaeva, who was not on friendly terms with her time, the poem introduces the tragedy of Lieutenant Schmidt. In Pasternak's poem it becomes a tragedy of an outstanding creative individual who dares to go against his time and is destroyed by it. In his speech at the trial, Schmidt connects his defeat with historical development in time:

[62] *Sočinenija*, I, 276.
[63] *Ibid.*, I, 457.

Как вы, я—часть великого
Перемещенья сроков,
И я приму ваш приговор
Без гнева и упрека.

Just as you, I am a part of a great
Displacement of dates,
And I shall accept your sentence
Without reproach or anger.

He sees not only himself, but also the judges who sentence him
to death, as the victims of the age in which they live: "Что
ж—мученики догмата, / Вы тоже—жертва века"[64] ("So,
martyrs of dogma, / You too are victims of your time").
Schmidt visualizes his own death as a boundary between two
different epochs:

Я знаю, что столб, у которого
Я стану, будет гранью
Двух разных эпох истории,
И радуюсь избранью.[65]

I know that the post by which
I will stand, will become a boundary
Of two different historical epochs.
And I rejoice at having been chosen.

Although Schmidt is defeated by his time, his failure marks the
end of an epoch. At the end of his life Pasternak's opinion of
his own relationship with his time was not only similar to
Schmidt's, but, curiously, has been at a later date recorded in
precisely the same words: "As he put it, he was the boundary
post between two epochs."[66]

In the novel in verse, *Spektorsky*, the conflict of a creative
individual with his time is less violent. The protagonist realizes
that his way of life and emotions are considered outmoded:

[64] *Ibid.*, I, 171–72.
[65] *Ibid.*, I, 173.
[66] Yevgeny Yevtushenko, *A Precocious Autobiography*, trans. Andrew R.
MacAndrew (New York: Dutton, 1964), p. 107.

"… ты и жизнь—старинные вещицы, / А одинокость—это рококо"[67] ("you and life are antique pieces / And loneliness is rococo"). A mood of acceptance and resignation is evident in the introduction to the novel. The author shares the emotions of the protagonist: he is conscious of his estrangement from the life around him and sees no reason for a change:

> Чужая даль. Чужой, чужой из труб
> По рвам и шляпам шлепающий дождик,
> И отчужденьем обращенный в дуб,
> Чужой, как мельник пушкинский, художник.[68]

> Alien distance. Alien, alien rain,
> Splashing from the drain pipes
> Into ditches and onto hats.
> And an artist, turned into an oak tree by his loneliness,
> Alien, like Pushkin's miller.

The poet is as isolated as the miller in Pushkin's "Rusalka" for whom all communication lines with the outside world are severed.

Early in the novel Spektorsky's sister attacks him for his aloofness and generally apolitical attitude:

> Вот видишь ли, ты—молод, это плюс,
> А твой отрыв от поколенья—минус.
> Ты вне исканий, к моему стыду.
> В каком ты стане?[69]

> You are young, you see, and that's an advantage,
> But your detachment from your generation is not.
> You are not involved, I am ashamed to admit.
> What camp do you belong to?

A similar attack is leveled at him by Olga Bukhteeva, his lover in Chapter Two, who reappears quite unexpectedly at the very end of the work. Her revolver, leather jacket, and the

---

[67] *Sočinenija*, I, 309.
[68] *Ibid.*, I, 278.
[69] *Ibid.*, I, 289.

declaration: "Я дочь народовольцев" ("I am a descendant of the People's Will Party") are meant to crush Spektorsky, who in 1919 is just as remote from politics as he had been in 1913. The fleeting impression of him that goes through Bukhteeva's mind: "Мой друг, как ты плюгав!"[70] ("My friend, how shabby you look") sums up his position in life as judged by "leather-jacket" standards and identifies Sergey Spektorsky as a direct forerunner of Yury Zhivago. Spektorsky does not argue with his sister; his answer implies that he could defend his position if he chose. In the encounter with Bukhteeva, although it is mentioned that he replies to her, it is only her words that are given. The only character in the novel who understands Spektorsky and with whom he shares his estrangement from society is another poet, Maria Ilyina. By 1919 (Chapter Nine) Maria is abroad. Thinking of her at that time, Spektorsky asks himself: "Где она—сейчас, сегодня? / ... / Счастливей моего ли и свободней, / Или порабощенней и мертвей?"[71] ("Where is she now, today? / ... / Is she happier and freer than I, or more enslaved and more dead?"). In her letters of the late twenties Tsvetaeva writes of her loneliness, of the lack of friends who appreciate poetry. Comparing her own fate with Pasternak's, she is convinced that Pasternak is happier because, living in Moscow, he must have friends for whom poetry is the most important concern of their life.[72] Spektorsky's question—if we take it as Pasternak's reply to Tsvetaeva—does not indicate that he agreed with her on this point.

In a poem to Tsvetaeva published in 1929 ("Ты вправе вывернув карман" ["You have a right, having turned your pocket inside out"]), Pasternak stresses the poet's rightful lack of concern for the transitory phenomena around him. It does not matter whose conversations he hears ("Мне все равно, чей разговор / Ловлю, плывущий ниоткуда" ["It does not matter whose conversation / I hear, that floats in from

---

[70] *Ibid.*, I, 315.

[71] *Ibid.*, I, 313.

[72] "Pis'ma Mariny Cvetaevoj," *Novyj Mir*, No. 4 (1969), p. 196.

nowhere"]) or what the fashions are at the time ("Мне все равно, какой фасон / Сужден при мне покрою платьев" ["It does not matter what style / Of dress is fashionable in my time"]). This indifference stems from a realization that *every* occurrence as such harbors poetry ("Любая быль—как вешний двор, / Когда он дымкою окутан" ["Every occurrence is like a backyard in springtime / When it is enveloped with mist"]). Despite his visible lack of concern for the immediate surroundings, the poet is bound to his time by an indestructible bond; the time itself "clings" to the poet: "И век поэта льнет к поэту"[73] ("And the poet's time clings to the poet").

Irrespective of the actual fate and circumstances of his life—such, for instance, as the place where he lives (Pasternak in Moscow, Tsvetaeva in Paris)—the poet is connected with his epoch and this cannot be altered. Later generations will not only associate the poet with his time, but will refer to the epoch itself by the poet's name:

Он вырвется, курясь, из прорв
Судеб, расплющенных в лепеху,
И внуки скажут, как про торф,—
Горит такого-то эпоха.[74]

It will break out, smoking, from the bottomless pits
Of the destinies, crushed into a flat cake.
And the grandchildren will say, as if of peat,
The epoch of so-and-so is on fire.

Pasternak speaks of this visibly reversed relationship between the poet and his time in "Lofty Malady":

Всю жизнь я быть хотел, как все,
Но век в своей красе
Сильнее моего нытья
И хочет быть, как я.[75]

[73] *Sočinenija*, I, 225. The last line quoted appears as a variant only in *Stixotvorenija*, p. 646.
[74] *Sočinenija*, I, 225.
[75] *Ibid.*, I, 268.

All my life I wanted to resemble everyone else,
But my time in its beauty
Is stronger than my whining
And wants to resemble me.

The same idea underlies Pasternak's view of the resemblance
between Mayakovsky and the Soviet state. It was so startling
that they could be taken for twins; and it was the state that
resembled the poet.[76] Likewise, Moscow at the time of World
War I appeared to Pasternak identical with Mayakovsky's
voice. Pasternak emphasizes that this was that similarity which
"ties together ... an artist with life, a poet with his time."[77]

Pasternak does not doubt the fate of his poetry; no matter
how incomprehensible and remote it might appear to his contemporaries, it belongs to *their* time. It is the Moscow of the
twentieth century that lives in his work:

Опять опавшей сердца мышцей
Услышу и вложу в слова,
Как ты ползешь и как дымишься,
Встаешь и строишься, Москва.

И я приму тебя, как упряжь,
Тех ради будущих безумств,
Что ты, как стих, меня зазубришь,
Как быль, запомнишь наизусть.[78]

With the slackened muscle of my heart
Again will I hear and put into words
O Moscow, your spreading out and smoking,
Your rising up and being built up.

And I will accept you as a harness,
For the sake of those future ravings,
[So] that you will learn me by heart as a poem,
Will memorize me as an actual fact.

The poet knows that his work cannot be crossed out and
forgotten; irrespective of the opinion of his contemporaries,
time will preserve his art:

[76] *Ibid.*, II, 293.   [77] *Ibid.*, II, 279.   [78] *Ibid.*, I, 321.

Жизнь моя средь вас—не очерк.
Этого хоть захлебнись.
Время пощадит мой почерк
От критических скребниц.   (1936)[79]

My life among you is not just a sketch.
There is enough of this to choke on.
Time will protect my handwriting
From the critical currycombs.

In *Doctor Zhivago* the feeling of organic ties between the poet and his time is stressed even more. Critical "currycombs" have no power over Zhivago's art because he does not publish and therefore does not depend on the contemporary critics. But despite his opposition to current tastes and views, as a poet Zhivago feels himself a part of the general development of human thought and thus not only a part of his time, but even an expression of the future: "At such moments Yurii Andreievich felt that the main part of the work was being done not by him but by a superior power which was above him and directed him, namely the movement of universal thought and poetry in its present historical stage and the one to come."[80]

In a poem written in 1921, Pasternak speaks of the true artists as being few and outwardly indistinguishable under the "grey crust" of current events, tastes, and values:

Нас мало. Нас может быть трое,
Донецких, горючих и адских
Под серой бегущей корою
Дождей, облаков и солдатских
Советов, стихов и дискуссий
О транспорте и об искусстве.[81]

[79] *Ibid.*, III, 6.

[80] *Ibid.*, IV, 448 (Hayward-Harari, p. 437). In *Povest'* the protagonist describes the art of his poet-improvisator as having almost prophetic qualities. It points the direction in which the sensibility of his audience will develop in the future (*Sočinenija*, II, 191–92).

[81] *Sočinenija*, I, 86.

We are few. Perhaps there are three of us
From the Don, inflammable and infernal—
Under the grey running crust
Of rains, clouds, and soldiers'
Councils, of verses and of discussions
About transportation and about art.

Although not understood and not even recognized by their contemporaries ("Вы поздно поймете"), they live on in their timeless art; as poets they are as permanent as life itself.

In "Lofty Malady," Pasternak reached a conclusion that poetry belonged to a sphere different from history. By virtue of his poetic gift, the poet is only a visitor, not a permanent inhabitant of this world. Under all social orders and economic systems the poet is someone who does not belong: "Гощу.—Гостит во всех мирах / Высокая болезнь"[82] ("I am a visitor. The lofty malady is a visitor in all worlds"). The same feeling of not belonging to the temporal world is repeated almost thirty years later in the poem "Ночь" ("Night," 1956), where the artist is implored to remain as alert as a pilot flying a plane over the sleeping world. The demand is justified by the disclosure of the artist's identity in the last stanza of the poem:

Не спи, не спи, художник,
Не предавайся сну,—
Ты—вечности заложник
У времени в плену![83]

Do not sleep, do not sleep, O artist,
Do not give in to sleep,
You are a hostage of eternity,
Kept prisoner by time!

The artist is kept hostage by time although by nature he belongs to eternity.

In a poem in *Second Birth*, the poem itself becomes a token of eternity brought into our temporal world:

[82] *Ibid.*, i, 267.
[83] *Ibid.*, iii, 82.

113

А в рифмах умирает рок
И правдой входит в наш мирок
Миров разноголосица.

И рифма не вторенье строк,
А гардеробный номерок,
Талон на место у колонн
В загробный гул корней и лон.[84]

And in rhymes fate dies,
And the diverse voices of the worlds
Enter as truth into our little world.

And rhyme is not the echoing of the lines,
But a cloak-room check,
A ticket for a place by the columns,
For the hum of roots and wombs beyond the grave.

The poet belongs to the two worlds: the eternal and the temporal; in his work the timeless beauty of life acquires flesh that unmistakably belongs to the time when the poet lives and writes.

[84] *Ibid.*, I, 341. In her book, Nadežda Mandel'štam speaks of this poem as evidence of Pasternak's desperate efforts to gain access to the Soviet literary establishment. This view—developed in a poem of Osip Mandel'štam's written in response to Pasternak's—seems to result from a curious misinterpretation of Pasternak's text. Pasternak's poem suggests that by means of poetry the poet gains entry to the "places of importance." According to Nadežda Mandel'štam, in this poem "the architecture of the main auditorium of the Moscow Conservatory is easily recognizable" (*Vospominanija*, p. 158). For her this signifies a poet's privileged position. In the context of the poem, however, it stands for an important place not in terms of Soviet reality, but in terms of eternity. The line following "Talon na mesto u kolonn"—"V zagrobnyj gul kornej i lon"—most unambiguously removes the situation from the level of governmental favors. The opposition is between our petty world, where people suffer even from love, and that authentic world where everything attains its true meaning. The Mandel'štams' misinterpretation obviously results from reading the "offending" phrase out of context.

THE POET AND OTHER PEOPLE

"The last year of a poet," according to Pasternak, is the time when—by being transformed into a permanent component of life—a poet becomes immortal. This period of transformation and attainment of immortality Pasternak visualizes as a liberation from our time. He describes it as a new and non-human youth; according to him, it is called "death" only for lack of a better name. Pasternak insists that it is not death, but immortality experienced here and now.[85]

Irrespective of the judgment of his contemporaries, an artist is ever reborn in the spirit of the following generations, when his time and contemporaries are dead. In "Безвременно умершему" ("To the Untimely Deceased"), a poem written in 1936 on the death of a young poet, Pasternak assures him that he will come back to life through his work:

Но тут нас не оставят.
Лет через пятьдесят,
Как ветка пустит паветвь,
Найдут и воскресят.[86]

But we will not be left here,
And after some fifty years—
Like a branch sprouting out—
We will be discovered and resurrected.

An artist's original perception of the world becomes a part of this world that remains after his death. Upon hearing the news of the suicide of his friend, the Georgian poet Paolo Yashvili, Pasternak suddenly recognized him in the nature around him: "I saw pieces and patterns of his spirit and style: his grass and water, his autumnal setting sun, his silence, his dampness and secretiveness. He would have said it precisely the way they glowed and hid, winked and died down. The sunset

---

[85] *Sočinenija*, II, 286.
[86] *Ibid.*, III, 8.

hour appeared to be either imitating him or recreating him from memory."[87]

The idea of a poet's becoming a part of life and nature upon his death Pasternak shares with Rainer Maria Rilke, whose influence he acknowledged as one of the most significant and lasting in his life. In his *Requiem*, which Pasternak translated in 1929, Rilke interprets a young poet's suicide as the fulfillment of his wish to become a part of life:

Ты там мечтал попасть
в живые недра дали, постоянно,
как живопись, дразнившей зренье здесь
и, очутившись изнутри в любимой,
сквозь все пройти, как трепет скрытых сил.[88]

A poem written on the death of an artist in 1931 indicates that for Pasternak it is not only an artist's work but also his relations with other people that assure his immortality:

Но он был любим. Ничего
Не может пропасть. Еще мене—
Семья и талант. От него
Остались броски сочинений.[89]

But he was loved. Nothing
Can be lost. Least of all
One's family and talent. There remain
The sketches of his compositions.

Here Pasternak refers to immortality as something modest and

[87] Pasternak's letter of August 28, 1937, to Paolo Jašvili's widow, Tamara Jašvili. Published in *Literaturnaja Gruzija*, No. 7 (1964), pp. 88–89 (hereafter cited as *LG*).

[88] Pasternak's translation of *Requiem*, "Für Wolf Graf von Kalckreuth," *Zvezda*, No. 8 (1929), p. 167. In the original, this passage reads as follows: "Dir schien, / dort drüben wärst du innen in der Landschaft, / die wie ein Bild hier immer vor dir zuging, / und kämst von innen her in die Geliebte / und gingest hin durch alles, stark und schwingend" (*Gesammelte Gedichte* [Insel Verlag, 1962], p. 415).

[89] *Sočinenija*, I, 355.

everyday (*вседневное наше бессмертье*). This view becomes very important in *Doctor Zhivago*.

Both for Yury Zhivago and his uncle Nikolay Vedenyapin, immortality in general—not only of creative artists—is life in other people. For Vedenyapin the most important aspect of the Gospels is not their moral teachings, but the fact that they are presented as parables from everyday life: "The idea that underlies this is that communion between mortals is immortal."[90] In the opinion of Zhivago, individual immortality depends on surviving in the memory of other people: "You in others—this is your soul. This is what you are. This is what your consciousness has breathed and lived on and enjoyed throughout your life—your soul, your immortality, your life in others. And what now? You have always been in others and you will remain in others. And what does it matter to you if later on that is called your memory? This will be you—the you that enters the future and becomes a part of it."[91] Everyday relations with other people play a role of supreme importance.

Over the years Pasternak was repeatedly accused of lacking concern for "other people" and of not sharing in the interests of "the people" (*народ*) as a whole. His poetry has been labeled "antidemocratic" and "antisocial" even by serious Soviet critics.[92] Although a lyric poet's preoccupation with himself and his emotional experiences in his verse follows from the definition of lyric poetry and hardly needs any theoretical justification, the literary climate in the Soviet Union was such that by 1927 Pasternak felt obliged to defend in print his interest in his own person. In a short untitled statement published in the journal *На Литературном Посту* under the

[90] *Ibid.*, IV, 42.

[91] *Ibid.*, IV, 68 (Hayward-Harari, p. 68).

[92] See, for instance, V. Aleksandrov, "Častnaja žizn'," *Literaturnyj Kritik*, 3 (1937), pp. 55–81; A. Ležnev, "Boris Pasternak," *op.cit.*, pp. 32–54. For the attacks in *Literaturnaja Gazeta* in the thirties, see O. Vojtinskaja, "Vraždebnye vlijanija v poèzii" (May 30, 1937); Dž. Altauzen, "Ne otstavat' ot žizni" (February 26, 1937); and an article by Ja. Èjdel'man on March 5, 1937. For a discussion of the attacks in the forties see Struve, *Russian Literature under Lenin and Stalin*, pp. 347 and 355.

general heading "Our Contemporary Writers about the Classics," Pasternak wrote: "The possibilities of an artistic method are never drawn from the *study* of contemporary life. Every one of us is connected with it functionally. This relationship could be also discovered by *analyzing* contemporary life, but—instead of listing by name all living mankind and among them chancing upon himself—it is easier and more reasonable for the poet to begin with himself."[93]

Although the theme of "other people" and their importance for the poet does not have much prominence in Pasternak's work before the mid-thirties—and in *Safe Conduct*, in the description of the newly discovered reality of the young poet Pasternak, people are placed on a par with "birds, houses and dogs, trees, and horses, and tulips"[94]—it would be unfair to think that "other people" had no place in his poetic world before that time. In "Childhood of Luvers" (1918), the spiritual aspect of the protagonist's growing-up process is presented as a function of her new awareness of other human beings and their value.[95]

In a consideration of the problem of "other people" in Pasternak's work, several aspects have to be pointed out. Among these are the poet's attitude toward the lower social strata of society and toward the intelligentsia and, on a different level, a development from the preoccupation with "the people," the abstract *народ*, to that with concrete human beings, *люди*, making up the people.

In 1943 in his comments on translating a Czech poet, Ondra Lysohorský, Pasternak speaks of a low social origin as an added asset: the range of possible development is practically unlimited, and the results attained are more valuable.[96] In a poem written in 1936 he calls fortunate those who by birth belong to the simple and the poor. Acknowledging that he himself *does not belong* to the people (*народ*) Pasternak

[93] *Sočinenija*, III, 159–60. Italics mine.
[94] *Ibid.*, II, 238.
[95] *Ibid.*, II, 111, 135–36.
[96] *Ibid.*, III, 179.

stresses, however, that as a poet he *depends* on the people:

Ты без него ничто.
Он, как свое изделье,
Кладет под долото
Твои мечты и цели.[97]

You are nothing without it.
It places your aims and dreams
Under the chisel
As if they were its own handicraft.

Although the sincerity of Pasternak's statement here cannot be questioned, the poem is not very convincing and cannot be counted among his best. Pasternak himself knew this. In February of that year he predicted that for a period of time his work would be poor.[98] In October, after the publication of the cycle "Путевые заметки" ("Travel Notes"), which includes the poem quoted above, he criticized it harshly: "Where do this water and dullness, and this lack of spirit, and stupidity come from ... ?"[99] For all its candor and directness this poem does sound like a theoretical statement about that abstract *народ*, in the name of which the Russian nineteenth-century intelligentsia struggled and made sacrifices and which remains in the headlines of Soviet propaganda until this day. The theoretical and abstract nature of the poem becomes especially clear when compared with "На ранних поездах" ("On Early Trains"), a poem written in 1941. The poet is overwhelmed by his own love and tenderness for the Russian people, represented by concrete human beings:

Сквозь прошлого перипетии
И годы войн и нищеты
Я молча узнавал России
Неповторимые черты.

[97] *Ibid.*, III, 11–12.
[98] *Ibid.*, III, 222.
[99] "Pis'ma druz'jam," *LG*, No. 1 (1966), p. 83.

Превозмогая обожанье,
Я наблюдал, боготворя.
Здесь были бабы, слобожане,
Учащиеся, слесаря.[100]

Through the troubles of the past
And the years of wars and poverty
I was silently getting to know
Russia's unique features.

Overcoming adoration,
I watched, worshipping.
There were peasant women here, country folk,
School children, locksmiths.

Here not only the thought, but the experience itself, is genuine.

In "Dawn", a poem of the Zhivago cycle, the poet does not speak of the people as representatives of lower social classes, but as human beings irrespective of their origin. In the original this is conveyed by the distinction between народ and люди. The poet's desire to be with the people eliminates the question of their social origin: "Мне к людям хочется, в толпу, / В их утреннее оживленье" ("I want to be with people, in a crowd / With its morning animation"). The poet experiences communion with all the people around him; he lives their life: "Я чувствую за них за всех, / Как будто побывал в их шкуре"[101] ("I feel for them all, / As if I had spent time in their skin").

In *Doctor Zhivago*, however, it is not only the protagonist's recognition of other people but his pronounced preference for the society of the uneducated to that of his peers that has to be considered. Returning to Moscow in 1922, Zhivago looks like a "peasant Seeker after Truth."[102] His only significant association is with Brykin, the young country boy, whom he meets on the way to the Urals and with whom he returns to Moscow. He marries the daughter of the former yardkeeper of the house

---

[100] *Sočinenija*, III, 28–29.
[101] *Ibid.*, IV, 557.
[102] *Ibid.*, IV, 478 (Hayward-Harari, p. 466).

where he grew up. This development cannot be explained satisfactorily by his mental or spiritual degradation, since Pasternak insists on the significance and the value of his writings. Neither can it be considered exclusively as the result of his circumstances or chance. Zhivago's conscious shunning of the company of his old and faithful friends, now university professors, Gordon and Dudorov, is undeniable.

For this professed rejection of the intelligentsia, Pasternak has been taken to task by Nadezhda Mandelstam in her *Reminiscences*. Although it is a mistake to identify the author with the protagonist of his work, there is no doubt that Pasternak shared many of Zhivago's views, and Zhivago's inclination to avoid the intellectuals should not be dismissed as insignificant for Pasternak himself. Perhaps without realizing it, Nadezhda Mandelstam herself provides an explanation of Zhivago's negative attitude. In her comparison of the simple, uneducated workers among whom she lived after her husband's arrest and the intellectuals, the former fare much better. In her opinion, being less dependent on the state they were able to preserve their spiritual freedom to a greater degree than were intellectuals. This observation reflects one of the fundamental laws of Soviet society: the relative freedom of an individual increases in direct proportion to his remoteness from the centers of power.

Zhivago appraises the post-revolutionary intellectuals the way Nadezhda Mandelstam does. He sees how average and commonplace the Soviet intellectual elite is: "Both Gordon and Dudorov moved among cultured academicians, they spent their lives among good books, good thinkers, good composers and good music, which was as good yesterday as today (but always good!), and they did not know that the misfortune of having average taste is a great deal worse than the misfortune of having no taste at all."[103] Later in this scene it is stated that Zhivago "could not bear the political mysticism of the Soviet intelligentsia, though it was the very thing they regarded as

[103] *Ibid.*, iv, 492–93 (Hayward-Harari, p. 481).

121

their highest achievement, or as it would have been called in those days, 'the spiritual ceiling of the age.'"[104]

Disillusionment with the intelligentsia was not something new for Pasternak at the time of writing *Doctor Zhivago*. In "Lofty Malady" (1923, 1928), he had very harsh and ironic words for the intellectuals and their role in the Revolution:

А сзади, в зареве легенд,
Дурак, герой, интеллигент
В огне декретов и реклам
Горел во славу темной силы,
Что потихоньку по углам
Его с усмешкой поносила
За подвиг, если не за то,
Что дважды два не сразу сто.
А сзади, в зареве легенд,
Идеалист-интеллигент
Печатал и писал плакаты
Про радость своего заката.[105]

And in the background, in the glow of the legends,
There was the fool, the hero, the intellectual
Burning in the fire of decrees and slogans
In the name of the glory of a sinister power,
That abused him in out-of-the-way places, quietly,
With a smirk, for his heroism, or because
Two times two does not at once make a hundred.
And in the background, in the glow of the legends,
The idealist-intellectual
Printed and composed posters
About the joy of his own decline.

Pasternak's denunciation of intellectuals here is not the same, however, as the denunciation for weakness and inefficacy, a charge that was officially propagated and widely spread after the Revolution. Pasternak's criticism is for the intelligentsia's

[104] *Ibid.*, IV, 494 (Hayward-Harari, p. 482).
[105] *Ibid.*, I, 480.

role in the Revolution and for its subsequent inability to acknowledge its failure of judgment. Likewise, it is the intelligentsia's attempts to rationalize rather than to admit its failure that cause Zhivago's contemptuous view of his intellectual friends.

Ascribing great importance to other people in the life of an individual does not, however, deprive Pasternak of the ability to assess his fellow humans in a rather realistic and down-to-earth way. In the poem "Перемена" ("Change"), published in 1958, Pasternak sums up his feelings on the subject. Retrospectively, he explains his original attraction to the people of the lower social strata not because of his lofty ideals, but because of the simplicity of their life:

> Я льнул когда-то к беднякам—
> Не из возвышенного взгляда,
> А потому, что только там
> Шла жизнь без помпы и парада.

> There was a time when I clung to the poor—
> Not because of an idealistic view
> But because only there
> Life went on without pomp and dressing-up.

After that time his views underwent a significant modification. During post-revolutionary times it became fashionable to act in an optimistic manner and to pretend that there was no sorrow in life. Poverty and misery were looked upon as personal shortcomings. The poet did not escape this generally corrupting attitude:

> И я испортился с тех пор,
> Как времени коснулась порча
> И горе возвели в позор,
> Мещан и оптимистов корча.

> And I became corrupted
> After our time had been touched with corruption,
> And misery had been equated with disgrace,
> And people tried to act optimistic and middle-class.

123

This realization calls forth a tragic note rarely found in Pasternak:

Всем тем, кому я доверял,
Я с давних пор уже неверен.
Я человека потерял,
С тех пор, как всеми он потерян.[106]

For a long time I have been unfaithful
To all those whom I trusted,
I lost [humanity in] man
After it had been lost by everyone.

The criterion that determines Pasternak's attitude toward others depends as much on himself as on the "other people." The relationship is better elucidated in Pasternak's discussion of the mutual interdependence between the poet and his readers.

Pasternak demands an ability to act as an individual, to judge for oneself, not only of a poet, but of a reader as well. In his early essay "Wassermann Test" (1914), Pasternak speaks of lack of individuality as particularly menacing in "our times." As a matter of fact, he defines "our times"—the time of democracy and technology—as an epoch that regards the phenomenon of individual talent as a dangerous superstition. "A democratization of demand," in Pasternak's opinion, has reduced the importance of the personal element in art.

Pasternak blames the reader for approaching new works of art with a preconceived and rigid scale of values based on extra-artistic qualities. He contemptuously divides the reading public—the "consumer crowd"—in two groups, both of which base their judgment of a work of art solely on the date of its appearance. One group rejects everything new, just because it is new; the other accepts it for the very same reason.[107]

Despite its polemic tone—this essay was written at the time of bitter strife among various futuristic groups—there is much in it that remained essential for Pasternak's later views.

---

[106] *Ibid.*, III, 66–67.
[107] "Vassermanova reakcija," *op.cit.*, pp. 33–38.

Although he takes an obviously negative and contemptuous attitude toward "the crowd," Pasternak defines it as "spiritual proletariat," thus dismissing social and economic considerations as completely superfluous.

The basis for the differentiation between "spiritual proletariat" and what by implication should be termed "spiritual aristocracy" is discussed in *Safe Conduct*.[108] The essential factor for this differentiation, according to Pasternak, is the individual's response to life. The ability to comprehend the language of poetry—in other words, to become an "initiate"—depends on the individual himself. Like the symbolists, Pasternak emphasizes the importance of an individual in art, but unlike them he places the responsibility on every individual rather than on a select few.

Although the similarity with the symbolists appears important, the difference is more crucial. According to Vyacheslav Ivanov, for instance, the language of true poetry is comprehensible only to the poet-priest and is entirely inaccessible to the crowd. Ivanov was able to discern mutual comprehension between the poet and the crowd in the distant past and visualized it as a desirable and probable achievement in the future. His crowd is helpless and faceless; the chasm between the poet of the new times and the crowd is tragic, but it is only some future development that conceivably might bring about a change in this situation. The accomplishment of the change, however, is beyond the control of the individuals.[109] Pasternak's crowd, on the other hand, is composed of individuals who *individually* bear responsibility for not understanding the poet. Thus Pasternak retains the symbolist view of the importance of a creative individual, but attributes the attainment of this lofty state not to some uncontrollable forces but to the individual's choice and effort. The appellation itself is not retained for creative artists only, but is applicable to every human being.

[108] *Sočinenija*, II, 206.

[109] Vjačeslav Ivanov, "Poèt i čern'," *Po zvezdam* (Peterburg: Ory, 1909), pp. 33–42 (first published in *Vesy*, No. 3 [1904]); "Zavety simvolizma," *Apollon*, No. 8 (1910), pp. 5–20.

Although Pasternak's tone is much milder in *Safe Conduct*, the essentially negative attitude expounded in "Wassermann Test" toward an uncreative reader is retained. Mentioning his conscious avoidance in his autobiography of some aspects and facts of his early life, Pasternak explains that he is more concerned with an integrated whole than with the isolated elements. He suspects, however, that the reader would have enjoyed those facts best of all, because he is attracted to that which does not exceed the limits of his own experience. For this type of reader history is a never-ending tale, whereas for Pasternak himself integration and synthesis are basic both to individual life and to history.[110]

It is also in *Safe Conduct* that Pasternak develops his conception of a creative relationship between the poet and his readers. A reader can be an active participant who by his creative effort continues the work of the poet. The subconscious of a genius cannot be measured, says Pasternak, for it includes his readers' creative reception, of which the poet himself is not aware. The essence of a poet's life, in his opinion, is not to be found on the usual biographical plane. It should be looked for under the names of his readers. Consequently, Pasternak's dedication of *Safe Conduct* to the memory of Rainer Maria Rilke is not a gift to him, but the evidence of the gifts that he received as Rilke's reader.[111]

The idea of a reader's creative response to a literary work also underlies Pasternak's conception of artistic translation. The author of a translation should first of all be a creative reader of the work he intends to translate.[112]

In 1928, Pasternak stressed that he had a high opinion of his own readers and expected them to comprehend his work without his assistance: "And now as regards the reader. I expect nothing from him and wish him a lot. The supercilious egotism, which underlies a writer's appeal to his audience, is alien to me, and passes my understanding. With his innate

[110] *Sočinenija*, II, 205.
[111] *Ibid.*, II, 213.
[112] *Ibid.*, III, 183.

golden faculty, the reader can always make out for himself what comes to pass in a book with things, with people, and with the author himself."[113]

The poet does not live and work in isolation from his readers. A mutual interaction between the poet and the reader had already been assumed in "Wassermann Test." It is only the indiscriminate and the uncreative reader, who chooses to stay within the limits of his past experiences and to avoid the unknown, whom Pasternak attacks. A creative reader is a participant in the poet's work and as such is a guarantee of his immortality.

[113] An article published in *Čitatel' i Pisatel'*, pp. 4–5, February 11, 1928. Reprinted as "Boris Pasternak o sebe i o čitateljax," with comments by Gleb Struve in *Grani*, 53 (1963), pp. 76–79. (Trans. by Gleb Struve, *Slavic Review*, XXIII [March 1964], p. 128.)

CHAPTER FOUR

The Responsibility of a Poet

"Цель творчества—самоотдача,
А не шумиха, не успех."

(*Сочинения*, III, 62

*"The purpose of creative work is the giving of oneself
Not the acclaim, not success."*

PASTERNAK repeatedly asserted that a poet is not free. In his early article "Black Goblet" (1916), the futurists were seen as carrying out the commands of their time.[1] In a poem in *A Twin in the Clouds*, reworked in 1929, the poet feels he is hired by someone mysterious for purposes unknown to him.[2] In his Chopin article (1945) Pasternak came to the conclusion that a realist by definition is not free.[3] The insistence that a poet has a duty to fulfill becomes stronger as the years go by and is most clearly expressed in Pasternak's statements about *Doctor Zhivago*. More than once he said that he had to write the novel, because he felt it his duty to be a witness to his age.[4]

This assertion of an artist's responsibility is coupled, however, with a most unambiguous defense of artistic freedom from any outside encroachments. One of Pasternak's pronouncements on the subject at a meeting of Moscow writers sounds unbelievably daring, considering that the year was 1936: "A writer cannot be presented with any demands, whether in the sphere of content or in that of form. A mother cannot be told: bear a girl, not a boy."[5] There is little doubt that the freedom that Pasternak attempted to retain as a Soviet

[1] *Sočinenija*, III, 149.
[2] *Ibid.*, I, 185.
[3] *Ibid.*, III, 172.
[4] See Ruge, *op.cit.*, p. 23; and Carlisle, *op.cit.*, p. 58.
[5] *Sočinenija*, III, 262.

writer was of a more profound variety than some of his colleagues from the Writers' Union were ready to grant him. The responsibility of the poet in Pasternak's interpretation is not to the powers within reach of the party policymakers in literature.

ON FAME AND MODESTY

Although it is true that *Safe Conduct* is not an autobiography in the usual sense of the word, Pasternak's statement in it that he is making use of his biography *only* in order to depict other people should not be taken at face value. Rather, he uses characterizations of other people to elucidate his own views and to point out changes in himself. Pasternak ascribed a special significance to his meeting with Vladimir Mayakovsky.

Pasternak's account of the impression that Mayakovsky and his poetry made on him is recorded in both of his autobiographies. The second version mostly supports the first, developing some of its points. In May of 1914, when Pasternak heard Mayakovsky read his tragedy "Vladimir Mayakovsky," he perceived certain similarities between Mayakovsky's and his own work. This realization led to a desire on his part to exclude a possibility of coincidences in the future. In *Autobiographical Sketch*, Pasternak specifies that the similarities were of technical nature ("similar construction of images," "similarity of rhyming") and admits that the "banality of coincidences," from which, according to *Safe Conduct*, he was trying to save Mayakovsky, was actually his fear of being taken for Mayakovsky's imitator. The description of Pasternak's reaction to the discovery of these similarities is the same in both versions: an attempt on his part to eradicate those inclinations which led to them.[6]

[6] Part Three of *Oxrannaja gramota* (*Sočinenija*, II, 265–93) is devoted almost entirely to Majakovskij; there are also passages about him in *Avtobiografičeskij očerk* (*Sočinenija*, II, 37–44).

According to Pasternak's accounts of his relations with Majakovskij in both works, there were two significant elements in his attitude toward

Majakovskij: an immediate recognition of Majakovskij's talent and a later rejection of his channeling and distorting his art in accordance with party directives. Pasternak's 1917 review of Majakovskij's book *Prostoe, kak myčanie* (1916), however, reveals that as early as 1917 he had not only high hopes for Majakovskij's future but some reservations as well. In this review Pasternak speaks of Majakovskij only "approaching poetry," predicts that he will have to sacrifice the "paradoxes of painting" upon achieving maturity, and tries to find an excuse for a desire to destroy or ignore tradition in the extreme acuteness of the experience of art, which eliminates from one's view everything else but the immediate vision of the artist. ("Kritičeskie ètjudy," *op.cit.*, pp. 18–19. According to Evgenij Pasternak's introductory note, the review, dated January 1917, was sent to Sergej Bobrov for the projected third issue of the Centrifuge almanac which never appeared. The manuscript of the review has been preserved in the archives of Sergej Bobrov.)

This review provides significant evidence against Pasternak's allegedly inexplicable change in attitude toward Majakovskij, of which he was accused after the publication of *Avtobiografičeskij očerk* (see, for instance, R. Wright-Kovaleva, "Vse lučšie vospominan'ja...," *Oxford Slavonic Papers*, XIII [1967], pp. 108–32). Strong personal attraction and recognition of Majakovskij's talent were from the very beginning combined with certain reservations about Majakovskij's art. Thus Pasternak's statements in *Avtobiografičeskij očerk* concerning Majakovskij should not be interpreted as a purely retrospective evaluation of their relations. In addition to the 1917 review, there is more evidence to support this view. *Oxrannaja gramota* indicates that there were some misunderstandings between the two as early as 1917. Pasternak speaks about the changes in himself connected with the writing of *Sestra moja žizn'* as occurring precisely at that time: the time of his second stay in the Urals (the review of Majakovskij's book was sent from the Urals). In 1923, Pasternak wrote his poem "Majakovskomu" as a dedication on a copy of *Sestra moja žizn'* (*Sočinenija*, III, 134). He quoted this poem in *Avtobiografičeskij očerk* (*Sočinenija*, II, 44) as evidence of their differences even in these early years. In his letter to Vjačeslav Polonskij (dated June 1, 1927, published in *Novyj Mir*, No. 10 [1964], pp. 195–96), announcing his final break with LEF, Pasternak readily admits that it is not easy for him and reaffirms his personal attraction to Majakovskij, but not without reservations: "Vy znaete, kak ja ego [Majakovskogo] ljublju i prodolžaju cenit'— *metafizičeskim avansom*" (p. 196; italics mine).

The best-known work of Pasternak's in which he speaks about Majakovskij is, undoubtedly, *Oxrannaja gramota*, the third part of which, dealing primarily with Majakovskij, was written under the impact of his death. Pasternak's feeling of loss and dismay at the poet's death overshadows his reservations. Nevertheless they are there: the account of the

At the source of the coincidences was the "romantic manner," the heroic tone that the two poets shared with most of the poets of their generation. "Romantic manner," according to Pasternak, although connected with certain technical devices, actually was an expression of a definite world view, inherited by Russian symbolists from the German romantics and passed on to the futurists.

The romantic manner, typical of the early Blok and intensified by Mayakovsky and Esenin, was characteristic of the period. Fusion of life and art was one of the cornerstones of the symbolists' world view and at the same time the source of the often tragic inability of symbolist poets to express themselves in their work. In the eyes of Blok's contemporaries, no one managed to achieve this fusion of life and art as fully as did he. It was said of Blok that he was not only a "natural symbolist" but himself a symbol. He was spoken of as a tragic actor playing himself. The resemblance of Blok the man to Blok the poet was so great that it created an almost eerie impression.[7]

---

misunderstanding between the two in 1917 and Pasternak's later inability to understand Majakovskij (*Sočinenija*, II, 284–85). *Oxrannaja gramota* was followed by a long period of silence: the thirties and the war, when Pasternak was publishing mostly translations, and when the past differences with Majakovskij were not important. The account in *Avtobiografičeskij očerk*, summarizing Pasternak's earlier views in a rather detached manner, appeared as a betrayal to many. Rita Wright-Kovaleva—one of those who cannot forgive Pasternak what he said about Majakovskij in *Avtobiografičeskij očerk*—fails to think of the intervening thirty years. Her memoirs consciously jump from the early twenties to the late fifties (*op.cit.*, p. 132). The source of Pasternak's detachment and apparent coldness to Majakovskij in the fifties is both in the original differences between the two and also in the intervening years, which produced the final perspective. Majakovskij's summing up of their attitudes, quoted by Pasternak in *Avtobiografičeskij očerk*, seems to be the best and the most concise characterization of their differences: "Nu čto že. My dejstvitel'no raznye. Vy ljubite molniju v nebe, a ja v èlektričeskom utjuge" (*Sočinenija*, II, 42–43).

[7] Innokentij Annenskij, "O sovremennom lirizme," *Apollon*, No. 2 (1909), p. 7. Boris Èjxenbaum, "Sud'ba Bloka," *Skvoz' literaturu* ('S-Gravenhage: Mouton, 1962), p. 219.

Blok himself spoke of his life turning into art and of himself as one among the "amazing puppets" of his art.[8] The earliest and most significant influence on Pasternak in this respect, even before Blok's, was that of Skryabin.

The romantic conception of a poet's life as a myth—which he himself creates and for which he pays with his own life—is convincing, claims Pasternak, only if viewed against a contrasting background. It presupposes the existence of the evil of mediocrity: "But outside the romantic legend this scheme is false. The poet placed at its foundation is inconceivable without non-poets, which serve as a background for him, because such a poet is not a living person engrossed in moral cognition but a visually biographical emblem, which requires a background to make its outlines visible."[9] Pasternak shared this view with the rest of his contemporaries and parted with it by giving up "romantic devices" and by shunning any poetization of his life that he considered false and pretentious. The immediate result of this change was the "non-romantic" poetics of his second book of verse, *Above the Barriers* (1917).

Further deliberations on acceptance or rejection of the romantic manner soon became irrelevant, as Pasternak explains, because in the poems of *My Sister, Life* the most non-contemporary aspects of poetry found their expression, and the poet realized that the force that was at the root of the book was more important than either the current poetic conceptions or the poet himself. The change that came about at the time of writing *My Sister, Life* Pasternak considered most important for his development as a poet. To use his own words, at this point in his life there occurred a total renunciation of the poet's life as a "visually biographical emblem," and a replacement by the life of a "living personality."

[8] "My own magic world became the stage for my personal actions, my 'dissecting auditorium' or ... the playhouse, where I myself was playing a role next to my amazing puppets. ... In other words, I had transformed my own life into art (a tendency very noticeable in the art of all European decadents). Life became art" (Aleksandr Blok, "O sovremennom sostojanii russkogo simvolizma," *Apollon*, No. 8 [1910], pp. 24–25).

[9] *Sočinenija*, II, 282.

In the passage in *Safe Conduct* where Pasternak describes those fundamental changes within himself, a reference to the *non-contemporary* aspects of poetry that he perceived during the revolutionary summer of 1917 is placed immediately after his comments on the *contemporary* view of the "biography of a poet as a spectacle." This suggests that the *non-contemporary* aspects of poetry, at least in part, were the opposite of the dramatization of the poet's life, i.e., the poet's desire to avoid displaying his life before the public. Pasternak somewhat elucidates this important point in his "posthumous" letter to Rilke. Trying to describe the essence of the Revolution as he saw it, he speaks of actuality taking over and crowding out "legitimate history." Pasternak experienced, during the summer of 1917, a realization that life as such was of foremost importance: "I saw a summer on earth that seemed to have recognized itself and that was as natural and prehistoric as a revelation."[10]

Characteristically, it was not the most obvious and easily discernible aspects of the Revolution that impressed Pasternak. *My Sister, Life*, the book which, in the poet's opinion, expressed everything "most unusual and imperceptible" about the Revolution, was considered by many critics not to contain anything pertaining to it. The upheaval, which caused the collapse of the long-established order, revealed to Pasternak the importance of life as such. From now on, an eternally young life was for him to be opposed to the imperfect and insecure creations of man—to the political and social institutions and systems. This experience, helped by Pasternak's natural inclination to avoid the limelight, deprived the romantic view of the poet (as secondary to life) of all its value in Pasternak's eyes.

"Образец" ("A Model"), a poem in *My Sister, Life*, juxtaposes the experience of the eternal and transient miracle of life and the generally prevalent current concern with the continued struggle:

[10] *Ibid.*, II, 345.

Все жили в сушь и впроголодь,
В борьбе ожесточась,
И никого не трогало,
Что чудо жизни—с час.[11]

Everyone lived parched and half-starved,
Hardened by the struggle,
And no one was moved
By the miracle of life that lasts only an hour.

In their concern for current events and developments, people forget about life itself. A sudden, lightning-like realization of the essence of life and life's response to his emotions led to the birth of the poet Pasternak on a summer morning of 1912 in Berlin. Now, in the midst of the events of the summer of 1917 in Moscow, this power asserted itself again, and the poet gave its name to the book he wrote at the time. From now on, the emphasis for Pasternak is invariably on poetry itself rather than on the poet.

A conscious avoidance of publicity becomes more pronounced as years go by; it is a subject to which Pasternak returns repeatedly beginning with the 1930's, but it is present in his earlier work as well. It is one of the points that illustrate the continuity of his views on the poet's position and role. But it has to be noted that, although Pasternak, from his early years, was opposed to publicity and to the romanticization of the poet's person and life, not only the forms in which this "romantic pose" manifested itself in literary life but even its causes were not the same at different times during his life.

In the summer of 1917, Pasternak renounced the "romantic pose" coming from the symbolists as something unsuitable to his temperament and his understanding of art. Very soon, however, he is showing resistance to a debased version of the same phenomenon—the "bohemian" attitude that vulgarized the romantic notion of the poet as an exceptional personality. According to the unwritten rule of this "popularized" approach,

[11] *Ibid.*, I, 15.

an artist had to dress, speak, and act like an artist. Pasternak's early story "Letters from Tula" (1918)[12] demonstrates very clearly what his poet is rejecting.

In the story, a young poet's abhorrence of "artistic" behavior leads him to a realization of a sharp distinction between the true and false in art. The false is represented by a group of movie actors and photographers. Their theatrically artificial behavior is not an individual aberration, however, but a reflection of the current attitude toward art and life. To his own dismay, the poet realizes that, by living at the same time with them, he shares something with the pretenders. The movie actors' "artistic" manner of behavior creates an atmosphere of parody and mockery not only of art but of life itself.

The young poet decides that conscience alone can distinguish between the true and the false both in life and in art. The realization that he is in Tula, "the location of Tolstoy's biography," gives a new meaning to the whole situation. He revolts against falsity and comes upon conscience as an antidote against pretentiousness, because he is in Tula on the "territory of conscience," where Tolstoy's extraordinary moral power deflects, like a magnetic field, the sensitive compass needle of the poet's soul. The poet vows to fight shallowness and pretentiousness in art even if he is left all alone in his fight. Pasternak dispatched his poet to Tula so as to motivate the reference to Tolstoy, who for him was a symbol of earnestness in art.[13] The young poet in the story comes to the conclusion that true art is hidden from the public eye; it is achieved in silence.

In "A Few Principles" (1922), Pasternak specifically objects to the contemporary tendency of art to display itself. He insists that art should be modest, should consciously try to conceal itself, and not suspect that it is visible even when hidden in the darkest corner.[14] Apparently it was not easy for Pasternak to keep his own life from turning into a spectacle.

[12] *Ibid.*, ii, 75–82.
[13] *Ibid.*, iii, 219.
[14] *Ibid.*, iii, 152.

In 1936 he defended his position of avoiding publicity, in this case manifested as a reluctance to give public recitals of his poetry. He mentioned the year 1922 as the time when he realized how false the easy "stage victories" were: "I sensed that I was faced with a possibility of developing some kind of a second life, repulsive in its cheap glitter, false and artificial, and this realization made me recoil from this path."[15] Recoiling from the phenomenon of stage reading—glorified by Maya-kovsky's practice, but irreparably degraded after him—Pasternak chose the difficulties of the invisible travel of the poet through his books.

Pasternak's refusal to give public recitals of his poetry was not only an expression of his personal predilection, but also a conscious resistance to the official practice of utilizing the popular romantic view of the poet for the purposes of the party. Stalin himself called Soviet writers "the engineers of human minds."[16] Accordingly, by the early thirties, the material well-being of writers was noticeably improved. For their privileged position they were expected to serve with their art the purposes of the party.[17]

The period after the First All-Union Congress of Writers in 1934 was especially difficult for Pasternak because his poetry was highly praised and set up as an example for other poets by Bukharin in his speech at the congress, and as a result—to Pasternak's great displeasure—his "fame" was, so to say, officially sanctioned. He wrote about this to his Czech translator in 1935: "All this time, beginning with the writers' congress in Moscow, I have had a feeling that, for purposes unknown to me, my importance is being deliberately inflated

[15] *Ibid.*, III, 220.

[16] Struve, *Russian Literature under Lenin and Stalin*, p. 256.

[17] See, for instance, Jurij Elagin, *Ukroščenie iskusstv* (New York: Chekhov Publishing House, 1952), and Nadežda Mandel'štam, *Vospominanija.* Although Elagin's book deals primarily with music and theater, it provides valuable information on the "taming" of literature as well. N. Mandel'štam gives a very vivid and convincing picture of the impossibility of physical survival for a poet in Soviet society if he continued to practice his art, but not according to the rules set up by the party.

(that is, artificially exaggerated), and all this by someone else's hands, without asking my consent. And I shun nothing in the whole world more than fanfare, sensationalism, and so-called cheap 'celebrity' in the press."[18]

In the thirties the bohemians of "Letters from Tula" had become members of the Writers' Union, professional writers and critics. The false and pretentious style not only remained typical of the times but was proclaimed the official style and was being imposed from above. In his published speeches and articles of the thirties, Pasternak consistently, and under the circumstances bravely, continued to express his opposition to this style, and even warned his colleagues against the temptations of the cheaply popular and the superficial in art.

In his speech at the First All-Union Congress of Writers in 1934 Pasternak urged his fellow writers not to sacrifice personality for the sake of status and warned them against the danger of becoming respected and esteemed dignitaries and thus ceasing to be writers.[19] This warning is strongly reminiscent of a similar warning by Blok in his 1921 Pushkin speech. The difference between Blok's and Pasternak's addressees, however, underscores the tragedy of a true artist in a totalitarian society. Although Blok addressed writers, he compared to Pushkin's "mob" (чернь) those officials who attempted to channel poetry, to encroach on its inner freedom.[20] Pasternak also addresses writers, but now they are taking upon themselves the functions of the censoring officials: the two have fused. A most tragic illustration of writers becoming state officials and fighting their own freedom is provided by the account of the attacks on Pasternak at the Moscow writers' meeting—nearly twenty-five years later—after he was awarded the Nobel Prize in 1958.[21]

[18] The letter is dated November 15, 1935. It was published in the Czech edition of *Oxrannaja gramota* (*Glejt*, Praha: Státní nakladatelství krásné literatury a umění, 1965). The letter appears between pp. 182 and 183.

[19] *Sočinenija*, III, 217–18.

[20] Aleksandr Blok, *Sobranie sočinenij*, VI, 167.

[21] "B. Pasternak i Sojuz Sov[etskix] Pisatelej" (Stenogramma), *Novyj Žurnal*, 83 (1966), pp. 185–227.

137

For Pasternak himself, a poet's right to obscurity eventually developed into his duty to remain unknown. The strongest indictment of publicity and fame is voiced in Pasternak's famous 1956 poem "Быть знаменитым—некрасиво" ("Being famous is unbecoming"). For the development and continuity of Pasternak's views on fame and obscurity, it is very significant that the 1956 poem expresses the same idea as another poem written twenty years earlier. The 1936 poem "Все наклоненья и залоги" ("All [grammatical] moods and voices") advises the poet: "Сгинь без вести, вернись без сил" ("Lose yourself without a trace, return exhausted"), and the 1956 poem: "И окунаться в неизвестность / И прятать в ней свои шаги" ("And to submerge oneself into obscurity, / And to hide one's steps in it"). Only his work will show what the poet actually accomplished during his lifetime: "И по репьям и по плутаньям / Поймем, кого ты посетил" ("We will make out by the burs / Whom you visited in your wanderings," 1936), and "Другие по живому следу / Пройдут твой путь за пядью пядь" ("On your fresh track, others / Will follow your path step by step," 1956). Modesty is an essential quality of the poet in both cases. Success is not the poet's aim; at best, it is only a side effect of his art:

Твое творение не орден:
Награды назначает власть.
А ты—тоски пеньковой гордень,
Паренья парусная снасть.[22]

Your creations are not an order of merit.
Awards are assigned by those in power.
But you are the rope of hempen yearning,
The sail-rig of soaring.

The 1956 poem expresses this idea more clearly:

Цель творчества—самоотдача,
А не шумиха, не успех.
Позорно, ничего не знача,
Быть притчей на устах у всех.[23]

---

[22] *Sočinenija*, III, 141.   [23] *Ibid.*, III, 62.

138

The purpose of creative work is the giving of oneself,
Not the acclaim or success.
It is shameful to amount to nothing and yet
To be a byword on everyone's lips.

Pasternak's views on fame were close to those of Rilke. In his book on Rodin, for instance, Rilke spoke of fame as "the sum of all the misunderstandings that gather about a new name."[24] In *Requiem für eine Freundin*, which Pasternak translated in 1929, the artist is spoken of as consciously shunning fame, trying to avoid its limelight.[25]

The highest degree of obscurity and disassociation from professional literary circles is achieved by Pasternak's poet in his last incarnation, in the character of Yury Zhivago. Only as a very young man is Zhivago associated with a student literary journal. In the course of the novel, when he writes down his poems, it is not with any plans of publication. Upon his return from Siberia, he manages to publish several books of verse and prose. He accomplishes this, however, privately, without the help of a publisher or a publishing house, and on a very modest scale. Zhivago's books have limited circulation, but are highly valued by discriminating readers. To his own surprise, Zhivago once learns that his reading public is not limited to those who know him personally and share his views.[26]

Despite his lack of connections with the official literary organizations and the apparent sacrifice of immediate success and therefore, it would seem, of a possibility of reaching his contemporaries, Zhivago's writings are not forgotten after his death but are read and cherished by his friends. In the epilogue of the novel, Gordon and Dudorov read Zhivago's poems from a notebook compiled by Evgraf Zhivago. This suggests that Yury Zhivago's works are circulated in manuscript.

For Pasternak himself such a degree of disassociation from the literary circles was unthinkable. Zhivago's situation

[24] Rainer Maria Rilke, *Selected Works*, Vol. I: *Prose*, trans. G. Craig Houston (London: The Hogarth Press, 1954), p. 95.

[25] Pasternak's translation was published in *Novyj Mir*, Nos. 8–9 (1929), pp. 63–69.

[26] *Sočinenija*, IV, 80, 486, 491.

probably reflects Pasternak's cherished but unattainable dream. Pasternak's relationship with such organizations was quite different. Until the end of his life he lived in his Peredelkino house, had an apartment in the Writers' House in Moscow, and, before his expulsion from the Writers' Union in 1958, was a member of that organization. Within those limits he tried to achieve a degree of inner freedom.

In the diary of the playwright Alexander Afinogenov, a friend and Peredelkino neighbor of Pasternak's in the thirties, we have the testimony of Pasternak's own indifference toward the immediate and official success of his work. With a note of admiration and slight surprise, Afinogenov wrote in 1937 that Pasternak was actually not concerned about the reception of his works. He was convinced that the real results of his efforts would become evident and properly appraised sometime in the future.[27]

Pasternak's attitude toward his public recitals of poetry remained consistently negative. In a letter written in 1959 he refuted as false a report that during World War II he recited poems to soldiers at the front. He wrote that even under normal conditions he was against public poetry reading, and that to give a recital at the front would be blasphemy. He admitted, however, that after the war he "was persuaded or induced to appear publicly ... in the concert halls of the rear."[28]

Throughout the years, Pasternak defended modesty and obscurity as the poet's way of life. The same attitude is forcefully and unambiguously reiterated in *Autobiographical Sketch*: "Life without privacy and without obscurity; life reflected in the splendor of a plate-glass show case is inconceivable to me."[29] Connected with this view is Pasternak's conception of the poet's life as self-sacrifice. This theme can be definitely discerned in his works of the late twenties; it becomes persistent beginning with the thirties.

[27] Aleksandr Afinogenov, *Stat'i, dnevniki, pis'ma, vospominanija* (Moskva: Iskusstvo, 1957), p. 152.

[28] "Three Letters to Stephen Spender," *op.cit.*, pp. 5–6.

[29] *Sočinenija*, II, 44. Translation is by D. Magarshack, *I Remember* (Pantheon, 1959), p. 101.

DESTINY OF A POET

Like Blok, Pasternak often used the image of stage acting as an allegory of human life. But if for Blok being on stage often meant clowning, for Pasternak it usually stood for assuming one's role in life and acting in accordance with it. The Blokian view of life as a harlequinade, however, appears in *Doctor Zhivago*. Soon after the Revolution, Zhivago notices how people around him are beginning to adapt themselves to one of two categories, that of "the moderates" or of "the politically advanced." Zhivago himself does not fit either category and is looked at askance by the members of both. At this time he begins a diary with the telling title "Playing at People" ("Игра в людей"). At the basis of this work is a realization that "half the people have stopped being themselves and are acting out who knows what."[30] Usually, however, Pasternak interprets acting as revealing rather than concealing the essence of life and reality.

Pasternak's frequent references to an individual's fate as an assumed role help to elucidate his favored paradox that dramatic acting is real life. In Pasternak's opinion, a true actor not only plays a role but lives it; he and his role merge. On the other hand, life itself, life off stage, is dramatic acting. Thus Pasternak divests acting of artificiality and make-believe; "acting" is not opposed to living one's real life. To act one's role means to be true to life. A free acceptance through an individual act of will underlies Pasternak's concept of "acting" one's life. Once a role is assumed, it is played to the end.

In Pasternak's first published prose work, "Apelles' Mark" (1915), the poet Enrico's eloquence causes the woman whom he is addressing to remind him jokingly that they are "not on stage." To this he retorts that life itself is acting, that people spend all their lives on stage, and that the natural behavior of a person, actually, is a difficult role that one plays all life long.[31]

In a poem written in 1928 and dedicated to Vsevolod Meyerhold and his wife, the actress Z. N. Raykh, Pasternak

[30] *Sočinenija*, IV, 188.
[31] *Ibid.*, II, 60.

speaks of the life of Adam and Eve as the first dramatic performance. In the Meyerholds' acting Pasternak perceived the same elements of truthfulness and natural dramatism as in the life of Adam and Eve. Paradoxically, the actor's make-up becomes his true self, his soul: "Вы всего себя стерли для грима. / Имя этому гриму—душа"[32] ("You have effaced yourself entirely for the sake of the make-up. / The name of this make-up is soul").

In the poem "Вакханалия" ("Bacchanalia"), *Когда разгуляется* (*When the Weather Clears*, 1959), the actress playing the part of Mary Stuart merges with the role:

То же бешенство риска,
Та же радость и боль
Слили роль и артистку,
И артистку и роль.

The same frenzy of risk,
The same joy and pain
Have fused the role and the actress,
And the actress and the role.

The creative power of the actress does not simply re-create a historical situation; on stage, in the person of the actress, Mary Stuart's life is lived again. Pasternak sees the creative energy of the actress as almost on the verge of succeeding in changing the actual fate of the heroine:

Словно буйство премьерши
Через столько веков
Помогает умершей
Убежать из оков.

As if the prima donna's rage,
After so many centuries,
Helps the deceased
Escape from her chains.

[32] *Ibid.*, I, 226–27. "Soul" in the last line might have a reference to the expression *igrat' s dušoj*, which implies becoming involved in one's role, living one's part.

This powerful acting of a talented actress in a Moscow theater is called forth by the more powerful acting of the historical protagonist. The realization of Mary Stuart's courageous acceptance of her role in life as her destiny and acting it to the end inspires the poet to one of his most spectacular verbal displays, one that utilizes the multiple meanings of the verb *играть*:

Сколько надо отваги,
Чтоб играть на века,
Как играют овраги,
Как играет река,

Как играют алмазы,
Как играет вино,
Как играть без отказа
Иногда суждено.

How much courage is needed
To act [so that it lasts] for centuries,
The way ravines and rivers
Surge with water,

The way diamonds
And wine sparkle.
The way one is sometimes destined
To act without fail.

Acting one's role in life is compared to various processes in nature. The verb *играть*, meaning both "to play" and "to act on stage," is used here in four instances idiomatically to describe natural phenomena: the upsurge of water in ravines and rivers, the play of light on diamonds, the fermentation and the sparkling of wine.[33]

---

[33] *Ibid.*, III, 96. Using a word both in a concrete and an abstract sense is one of the devices employed by Pasternak in his struggle against the automatization of language. It both attracts the reader's attention and amplifies the meaning of the word. The following two examples are from *Sestra moja žizn'* and *Temy i variacii*, respectively. In "Bros', k čemu švyrjat' tarelki, / Bit' trevogu, bit' stakany?" (*Sočinenija*, I, 28), the two

For Pasternak, an artist's destiny is similar to acting a difficult and responsible part. Speaking of the poet's destiny, Pasternak repeatedly returns to the image of acting on stage. The beginning of the poet's career is referred to as a "debut," the place where he has acquired his experience as an "arena."[34] In *Safe Conduct*, describing his giving up of the romantic view of the poet's life that inevitably leads to a tragic end (Mayakovsky and Esenin come to mind here), Pasternak suggests that he avoided this fate by abandoning this world view at a time when it still was "noncompulsory and mild ..., did not presume heroism and did not smell of blood."[35] As early as 1931—the year of publication of *Safe Conduct*—Pasternak wrote his famous and often-quoted poem about the "unheard-of simplicity," the practice of which will not gain favors for the poet but rather lead to consequences dangerous for him: "Но мы пощажены не будем, / Когда ее не утаим"[36] ("But we will not be spared, / Unless we conceal it").

The premonition of eventual reckoning has a more ominous note in "О, знал бы я, что так бывает" ("Had I known that this is what happens"), also written in 1931. A realization that verses have the power to kill their creator comes as a surprise:

О, знал бы я, что так бывает,
Когда пускался на дебют,
Что строчки с кровью—убивают,
Нахлынут горлом и убьют!
От шуток с этой подоплекой
Я б отказался наотрез.

---

meanings of *bit'* in line two are already suggested in line one by *švyrjat'*, pointing to the concrete meaning of *bros'*. In the other instance, the concrete and the abstract meanings of a word are not only juxtaposed but actually compared: "... ljubimuju *trogat'* / Tak, kak mne, ne dano nikomu. / Kak ja *trogal* tebja! Daže gub moix med'ju / *Trogal* tak, kak tragediej *trogajut* zal" (*Sočinenija*, I, 106).

[34] *Sočinenija*, I, 351; III, 3.
[35] *Ibid.*, II, 282.
[36] *Ibid.*, I, 328.

Had I known that this is what happens,
When I decided to make my debut,
That lines of verse are able to kill,
To choke you to death with blood,
I would have flatly refused
To take part in jokes with such implications.

Now it is the age of the poet that makes him realize the seriousness of the situation; and at this point the image of the poet "performing" his own life returns:

Но старость—это Рим, который
Взамен турусов и колес
Не читки требует с актера,
А полной гибели всерьез.

But old age is Rome, which
Instead of cock-and-bull stories
Demands not a run-through from an actor,
But total [self-] destruction—and in earnest.

Pretending will not do: the poet-actor has to give his life for his art. Blok, Esenin, Mayakovsky played their life tragedies before everyone's eyes. By preventing his life from becoming a legend and a myth, Pasternak was avoiding the tragic outcome of his contemporaries. To judge by these poems, however, it appears that by the early thirties it was clear to him that in the society in which he lived no degree of concealment could protect the poet who remained true to his calling. Paradoxically, by obeying the commands of his art, the poet crosses the border beyond which art has no power; it is the realm of life itself:

Когда строку диктует чувство,
Оно на сцену шлет раба,
И тут кончается искусство,
И дышат почва и судьба.[37]

[37] *Ibid.*, I, 351.

145

When emotion dictates a line,
It sends a slave onto the stage,
And art ends here,
And there breathe soil and fate.

A 1936 poem, "Мне по душе строптивый норов" ("I like [his] obstinacy"), recapitulates some of the points of the 1931 poem "Had I known that this is what happens." But whereas in the earlier poem the idea of the poet not being his own master is presented in its tragic aspect (the poem is written in the first person; its tone is personal and emotional), in the later poem the tone is calmer, and a note of acceptance is discernible (here the poet is spoken of in the third person). Having reached a high point in his artistic development, the artist intuitively avoids fame, is even ashamed of his own achievements, but realizes that he missed the moment when he could have hidden from the public eye; now he has to continue on his way.[38]

Pasternak returns to a comparison of a poet's life with a dramatic performance in "Hamlet," the opening poem of the Zhivago cycle. The poem begins with the hero as an actor entering on stage. The actor playing the role of Hamlet becomes Hamlet himself. In his notes to Shakespeare's tragedies, Pasternak interprets "Hamlet" as a tragedy of duty and self-denial. Once he realized for what role he was chosen, Hamlet could not have acted otherwise than he did. The acceptance of his role was a sign of his strength.[39]

Both the poem and the notes have direct references to Christ as the prototype of self-denying sacrifice and of carrying out the role, once assumed, to the end. In the notes, Pasternak speaks of Hamlet's realization that he has to fulfill "the will of him who sent him"; in the poem the words "Если только можно, авва отче, / Чашу эту мимо пронеси"[40] ("If it is

---

[38] *Ibid.*, III, 3.
[39] *Ibid.*, III, 195. Victor Frank has interpreted the entire *Doktor Živago* as Pasternak's version of Hamlet in "A Russian Hamlet: Boris Pasternak's Novel," *The Dublin Review*, September 1958, pp. 212–20.
[40] *Sočinenija*, IV, 532.

possible, Abba, Father / Let this cup pass from me") are a paraphrase of Christ's prayer in the garden of Gethsemane. Written in the first person, the poem superimposes Zhivago's own destiny over the destinies of Christ and Hamlet. Just like the two prototypes of self-denial referred to in the poem— after a momentary desire to change the outcome of the tragedy —the poet realizes that he cannot evade his destiny by rejecting his long-accepted role.

In Pasternak's late poetry "life for others" becomes an important theme. Life as sacrifice is the theme of a war poem "Смерть сапера" ("Death of a Sapper"). Selfless love is the *only* human experience that has a permanent value:

Всё в жизни может быть издержано,
Изведаны все положенья,—
Следы любви самоотверженной
Не подлежат уничтоженью.

Everything in life can be spent,
All situations experienced.
The residue of selfless love
Is not to be destroyed.

Self-sacrifice *is* the path to immortality:

Жить и сгорать у всех в обычае.
Но жизнь тогда лишь обессмертишь,
Когда ей к свету и величию
Своею жертвой путь прочертишь.[41]

To live and to burn out is everyone's custom.
But life becomes immortal
Only when your sacrifice traces for it
The path to light and sublimity.

Life as sacrifice is one of the central themes of *Doctor Zhivago*; it figures prominently in Zhivago's poems. In "Свадьба"

---

[41] *Ibid.*, III, 48.

147

("Wedding") life is referred to as a gift to others:

Жизнь ведь тоже только миг,
Только растворенье
Нас самих во всех других
Как бы им в даренье.[42]

But life is also only a moment,
Only the dissolving
Of ourselves in all others,
As if in gift to them.

In "Dawn" the poet speaks of life for others as a spiritual
victory for an individual:

Со мною люди без имен,
Деревья, дети, домоседы.
Я ими всеми побежден,
И только в том моя победа.[43]

With me are people without names,
Trees, children, stays-at-home.
I am conquered by all of them
And in this alone is my victory.

In "Хлеб" ("Bread," 1956), self-abnegation is a prerequisite
for happiness. The poem points to the Gospel parable (John
XII:24) of a seed dying and thus bearing fruit.[44]

This theme, however, was not new for the Pasternak of the
forties and fifties. In "Lieutenant Schmidt" the protagonist sees
his own role in the uprising as a sacrifice: "Я жил и отдал /
Душу свою за други своя"[45] ("I lived and gave / My life for
my friends"). The allusion to the Gospels (John xv:13) connects it directly with the character of Zhivago as Hamlet and
Christ. Schmidt's decision to head the uprising, knowing that

[42] *Ibid.*, IV, 543.
[43] *Ibid.*, IV, 558.
[44] *Ibid.*, III, 74.
[45] *Ibid.*, I, 162.

it is doomed to failure, is the only course he can take without going against his conscience.

A meaningful life is achieved only through self-sacrifice; this is especially true of the life of a creative artist. Self-sacrifice is an absolutely necessary ingredient of art and therefore the destiny of the artist. In his speech "О скромности и смелости" ("On Modesty and Courage"), delivered at the plenary meeting of the Board of the Writers' Union in February of 1936, Pasternak said that he could not conceive of art "without risk and spiritual self-sacrifice."[46] In a private letter written in 1950, he was more explicit: "I have in mind that which is most artistic in the artist—sacrifice, without which art is useless and scandalously nonsensical, and without which works of art are covered with a veneer of talent on the outside, but are held together by an idea that was known to and perhaps even superseded by mankind at the time of its emergence from a primitive state."[47]

Pasternak's conviction that it was his duty to write his novel and to have it published—a conviction that was not shaken either by his friends' negative appraisal of the novel, or by the difficulties and dangers that its publication brought to his life—is the most obvious example of this view applied to the poet's life.[48] The worldwide recognition and publicity that fell to Pasternak's lot during the last few years of his life, despite his undoubtedly sincere desire for obscurity, in a curious way brought about a realization of his favored image of an artist's life as a dramatic performance on stage.

The poet's desire for a modest life style was outweighed by a sense of responsibility as a surviving representative of a generation that was either destroyed physically or silenced and crushed spiritually. *Doctor Zhivago* appeared after years of near silence on Pasternak's part. For many years his translations were his only source of income; he depended heavily on

[46] *Ibid.*, III, 222.

[47] "Kraj, stavšij...," *op.cit.*, p. 187.

[48] For a detailed account of the events leading to and following the publication of the novel, see Robert Conquest, *The Pasternak Affair*.

them until the end of his life.[49] His isolation was only partly by choice: in his desire for obscurity Pasternak was helped by the official line of ignoring his work.

The turning point in Pasternak's own attitude toward official literature and his position in it has to be placed sometime in 1937. The well-known story of his refusal to sign the writers' statement approving the execution of the generals in 1937 is highly indicative of Pasternak's inability to comply with the demands placed upon writers in Soviet society.[50] Although, as it turned out later, this information never reached those who could have used it against the poet, this episode, considering the situation in Moscow in 1937, assumes symbolic significance. It was a refusal to accept the government's act of terror as just and thereby pronouncing a judgment on it, and as such it was an act of defiance on Pasternak's part and a testimony to his conscious challenge of the accepted and expected mode of conduct.

The year 1937—the peak of Stalin's terror—brought, among other things (such as the arrest of Bukharin, with whom Pasternak's name had been associated since the Writers'

[49] Pasternak's attitude toward translating was contradictory. Afinogenov noted in his diary in 1937 Pasternak's opinion about translating: "I would have achieved the same degree of success had I become a traveling salesman" (Afinogenov, *op.cit.*, p. 152). There are numerous negative references in Pasternak's letters of the fifties to translations taking time from his own work, but there is no doubt that translations served more purposes in his life than simply the pecuniary ones. (See Chapter Two. For Pasternak's comments in the fifties see Renate Schweitzer, *Freundschaft mit Boris Pasternak: Ein Briefwechsel* [Verlag Kurt Desch, 1963], pp. 101, 104; also Andrej Voznesenskij, "Nebo Borisa Pasternaka," *Inostrannaja Literatura*, No. 1 [1968], pp. 199–203.) On the other hand, he spoke of his translations of Shakespeare, Goethe, and a Georgian poet, Baratašvili, as significant accomplishments in his life ("Kraj, stavšij...," *op. cit.*, p. 192).

[50] The story is reported in Robert Conquest, *The Pasternak Affair*, pp. 41–42. See also Nadežda Mandel'štam, *Vospominanija*, p. 115. Pasternak's signature did appear, however, a year earlier under the letter of Soviet writers demanding capital punishment for the defendants in the Zinov'ev-Kamenev trial (published in *Pravda*, August 21, 1936).

Congress in 1934), the deaths of his two friends, the Georgian poets Paolo Yashvili and Titian Tabidze, both of whom were victims of the terror. These two, together with Marina Tsvetaeva, who returned to the Soviet Union in 1939 and hanged herself in 1941, are the "three shades" to whom the last chapter of *Autobiographical Sketch* is dedicated and of whose deaths Pasternak spoke as the greatest loss in his life. There is every reason to believe that these deaths contributed greatly to the changes in Pasternak.

His only letter from 1937 (among those published so far) is to Yashvili's widow. It was written after Pasternak had learned of Paolo's suicide: "The impact of this blow flung me far aside from everything in the city, from that which is unjustifiably loud, unnecessarily complicated, excitedly unconcerned, eloquently empty."[51] His letters to Tabidze's widow indicate that these changes were of a permanent nature. In 1944 he wrote of the effects of Titian's death on him: "The admission of this loss added something to my moral stature and made me silent and active as if I have become a kind of a 'brother of charity,' absorbed in my work and glum."[52] In 1955, when it was officially confirmed that Tabidze had been shot soon after his arrest in 1937, Pasternak returned to the subject again: "I have always sensed this terrible truth. This determined my views, my attitude toward our time and its major representatives, my destiny."[53]

In letters from 1938 and 1939 Pasternak indicates that his life is becoming increasingly difficult. As the reason, he gives his inability to be enthusiastic about current events. He admits that he never succeeded in attaining the proper degree of enthusiasm even before and adds that recently the notion itself became unendurable for him. There is a reference to "that time" (apparently 1937)—the time of "unbearable shame and

[51] Letter to Tamara Jašvili, *LG*, No. 7 (1964), p. 88.

[52] "Pis'ma druz'jam," *LG*, No. 1 (1966), p. 89.

[53] *Ibid.*, No. 2 (1966), p. 94. The change in Pasternak during the prewar years was noted by Kornej Čukovskij ("I obraz mira, v slove javlennyj ...," *Junost'*, No. 8 [1965], pp. 66–70).

misery," when he was ashamed to go on living, ashamed to move, to talk, to smile.[54]

A most poignant poetic expression of Pasternak's feelings as one who survived into the fifties is found in his poem "Душа" ("My Soul," *When the Weather Clears*). The poet sees his soul as an urn keeping the ashes of his friends:

Душа моя, печальница
О всех в кругу моем,
Ты стала усыпальницей
Замученных живьем.

....

Душа моя, скудельница,
Всё, виденное здесь,
Перемолов, как мельница,
Ты превратила в смесь.

И дальше перемалывай
Всё бывшее со мной,
Как сорок лет без малого,
В погостный перегной.[55]

O my soul, a mourner
For everybody in my circle,
You turned into a crypt
For all those tortured to death.

....

O my soul, a burial ground
That like a mill
Reduced to a mixture
Everything witnessed here.

Go on grinding
Everything that happened to me
Into a graveyard compost,
As you have been doing for nearly forty years.

[54] "Pis'ma druz'jam," *LG*, No. 1 (1966), p. 84, and "Kraj, stavšij...," *op.cit.*, p. 180.

[55] *Sočinenija*, ш, 63–64.

Pasternak's faithfulness to the memory of his contemporaries who did not survive into the fifties remained a significant part of his outlook, interests, and activity until the end of his life. Here again he differed fundamentally from his colleagues. On a personal level, for the majority of Soviet intellectuals de-Stalinization meant giving way to nostalgic reminiscing of the 1920's as a time when they were young and the full development of the totalitarian regime was divined by but a few. Pasternak's response—quite unusual in someone who personally went unscathed—was manifested in his unwillingness and inability to go on living and writing as he did before, as if nothing had happened. It was his conviction that a poet's duty is to change with changing life: "One must live without tiring, look ahead, be nourished by living resources." [56] Defending the changes in himself and in his art, Pasternak spoke of "heroic devotion to one's point of view" as lack of humility and insisted that he did not want to become "a slave to his own name." [57]

JOY OF EXISTENCE

In a letter from 1952 Pasternak noted his "unnatural" response to his friends' harsh criticism of his novel: "... I ... break into a smile, as if this abuse and criticism were praise." [58] This unconcern stems from a conviction that his critics missed the point. What he tried to accomplish in his novel was of utmost importance for Pasternak, and any criticism seemed petty in comparison with his feeling of a duty fulfilled. He wrote about *Doctor Zhivago*: "What I sought and pursued in the book while writing it, was to embody and to personify the astonishing, the undefinable (mysteriously making happy even

[56] *Ibid.*, II, 34.
[57] Carlisle, *op.cit.*, p. 54, and Nils Åke Nilsson, "Besuch bei Boris Pasternak," *Boris Pasternak. Bescheidenheit und Kühnheit* (Zürich, 1959), p. 107.
[58] "Kraj, stavšij...," *op.cit.*, p. 193.

in the sorrow) spirit of life (or perhaps the sense and feeling of courageous and humble life worship).["59] Being truthful to the spirit of life, which mysteriously makes one happy even in sorrow, is a prime responsibility of an artist. In 1922 Pasternak claimed that one thing that is unquestionably within the power of the artist is to avoid distorting the voice of life that he hears.[60]

In *Autobiographical Sketch*, Pasternak mentions as one of the essential points of his early paper "Символизм и бессмертие" ("Symbolism and Immortality") the conviction that the joy of existence experienced by an artist is immortal.[61] In 1935 he spoke of poetry as "organic function of happiness of man."[62] Zhivago comes to the conclusion that art in general (including tragic art) is a tale about the happiness of existence.[63]

The protagonist of *A Tale* (1929) experiences joy when one would expect him to be unhappy. He has just parted with the woman he loves, but his love leads him to a realization that the meaning of life is in life itself: "Everything in the world has been understood; there is nothing else to be understood. What remains is to live. ... What happiness!"[64] This is the same view as that of Zhivago: the meaning of life is in living, not in preparation for or contemplation of life.

The joy of existence causes Yury Zhivago to transcend the practical hardships he encounters in life. In Varykino, in a most hopeless situation and aware of the imminent dangers for Lara and himself, Zhivago is happy and feels undeserving of this happiness: "Lord! Lord! ... and all this is for me? Why hast Thou given me so much? Why hast Thou admitted me to Thy presence, allowed me to stray into Thy world, among Thy

---

[59] Quoted from Pasternak's letter (May 5, 1959) to Mrs. Beatrice Nosco. The original in English.

[60] *Sočinenija*, III, 153.

[61] *Ibid.*, II, 25–26. The paper was delivered in February of 1913 ("Ljudi i položenija," *Novyj Mir*, No. 1 [1967], p. 219). Manuscript lost.

[62] "Slovo o poèzii," *Sbornik statej, posvjaščennyx...*, p. 9.

[63] *Sočinenija*, IV, 466.

[64] *Ibid.*, II, 199.

treasures, under Thy stars. ..."[65] This closely paraphrases a passage from Pasternak's letter written in December of 1946. His inner happiness does not depend on external circumstances, to which he does not give much thought or attention: "How do we live? To be sure, not badly or, perhaps, not well at all—it is difficult for me to judge, because I am blinded by the inner happiness of my existence. ... Why, why am I so fortunate in this world, ... I am on the verge of tears, so startling and unfathomable is this."[66] A few years later he wrote, trying to sum up his life: "Now, I will die, but my life will remain, such a happy life, for which I am so grateful to Heaven."[67] This primacy of the joy of existence over actual occurrences is essentially the same as Pasternak's concern for "life as such" in the face of the revolutionary upheaval (see pp. 133–34).

With this overwhelming joy of existence is connected Pasternak's general optimism and his faith in the victory of good. In World War II he saw a dramatic change from the spirit of the prewar years; it was a fire that destroys evil and purifies that which is destined to survive.

The protagonist of the unfinished narrative poem "Зарево" ("A Glow of Fire," 1943) returns from the front a changed man:

Людей переродило порохом,
Дерзанием, смертельным риском.
Он стал чужой мышиным шорохам
И треснувшим горшкам и мискам.

People have been regenerated by gun powder,
By daring, by mortal risk.
He became a stranger to the rustle of mice,
And to cracked bowls and pots.

He senses the changes not only in individual people, but in the historical development of the country:

[65] *Ibid.*, IV, 448–49 (Hayward-Harari, p. 437).
[66] "Pis'ma druz'jam," *LG*, No. 2 (1966), p. 86.
[67] "Kraj, stavšij...," *op.cit.*, p. 189.

А горизонты с перспективами!
А новизна народной роли!
А вдаль летящее прорывами
И победившее раздолье![68]

And the horizons with such vistas!
And the newness of the people's role!
And the victorious freedom
That surges into the distance as a break-through!

This reflects a wide spread hope that victory in the war would bring radical changes for the entire Soviet system. In the poem, when he returns home, the soldier is confronted by the unchar,ged attitude of his wife; this saddens him but does not destroy his general optimism. Had Pasternak continued the poem, the disappointment was bound to become deeper and more significant; the soldier would have had to face not only his wife's pettiness and, possibly, unfaithfulness, but a continuation of Stalin's system of repression.

The feeling that life has to be different after the sacrifices of the war pervades the epilogue of *Doctor Zhivago*. Zhivago's friends, Gordon and Dudorov, agree that the war was an escape both for those within as well as for those outside the concentration camps. The reality of its horror was better than the prewar life of constant lies. It served as a liberation from the inhumanity of the "dead letter." For them the expectation of freedom is the only significant thing about the postwar years; Zhivago's book, which they are reading, supports their hopes.[69] Chronology provides an easy clue to this optimistic outlook. *Doctor Zhivago* was finished after Stalin's death, when the hopes for change were revived.

Although the liberalization of the post-Stalin years proved to be a temporary and partly reversible development (for Pasternak himself, the fifties turned out to be a time when official wrath was directed at him personally and in its vehemence exceeded anything that he had experienced before), he

[68] *Stixotvorenija*, p. 564.
[69] *Sočinenija*, IV, 519–20, 530–31.

insisted until the end that—despite appearances—there was a new era about to begin: "I have a feeling, that a completely new era is beginning with new tasks and new demands on the heart and on human dignity, a silent age that will never be proclaimed and allowed voice but will grow more real every day without our noticing it. That is why Dr. Zhivago is the most important piece of work I have been able to do so far in the whole of my life." [70]

Pasternak believed that both Russia and Western Europe were on the threshold of a new era. The preceding period, the technological age, had developed to the fullest and thus exhausted itself entirely; now it is time to move to something else. In the new period, the spiritual in man would gain ascendance over the physical. [71] The theme of the future conquering the past appears in his poetry:

Воспоминание о полувеке
Пронесшейся грозой уходит вспять.
Столетье вышло из его опеки.
Пора дорогу будущему дать. [72]

The memory of fifty years
Recedes like a storm that has just swept through.
The century is no longer under the guardianship
   [of those years].
It is time to give way to the future.

A recurrent image of spring, as the symbol of ever-returning life and its victory over death and evil, is another expression of Pasternak's optimism and faith in life. In Zhivago's poems the miracle of spring and the revival of nature are coupled with the resurrection of Christ. Despite the gloom and the darkness

[70] Pasternak's letter quoted in the editorial "A Man Alone," *Manchester Guardian*, LXXIX, No. 19 (November 6, 1958), p. 1. Nadežda Mandel'štam's cautious optimism evident in *Vospominanija* likewise stems from a conviction that since Stalin's death some irreversible changes have taken place in the people rather than in the system.

[71] Peltier-Zamoyska, "Pasternak, homme du passé?" *op.cit.*, pp. 23–25.

[72] *Sočinenija*, III, 106.

after His death, the faith of His followers carries them through to the resurrection.

In "Нобелевская премия" ("The Nobel Prize"), one of Pasternak's most frankly pessimistic poems, where a note of despair is unmistakable, he again expresses this optimistic faith in the final victory of good:

Но и так, почти у гроба
Верю я, придет пора—
Силу подлости и злобы
Одолеет дух добра.[73]

But even so, nearing my grave,
I believe the time will come
When the spirit of good will vanquish
The power of baseness and malice.

Characteristically, Pasternak puts his faith not in social systems and ideologies but in the spirit of good attainable by every human being:

Не потрясенья и перевороты
Для новой жизни очищают путь,
А откровенья, бури и щедроты
Души воспламененной чьей-нибудь.[74]

Neither cataclysms nor revolutions
Clear the path for new life,
But revelations, storms and the bounty
Of someone's soul set aflame.

Lara's immediate response to the catastrophic events of 1917 is a desire to entrust herself to life. The endless speechmaking of the revolutionary summer makes Zhivago long for deceptively silent and unobtrusive phenomena, first among which are nature and work.[75] As the years go by, Zhivago attaches more value to the simple things in life. Once, toward the end of his stay in the Urals, he is moved to tears by the purity of the snow outside and of the bed linen inside the house. At least one

[73] *Ibid.*, III, 108.   [74] *Ibid.*, III, 106.
[75] *Ibid.*, IV, 129, 141.

critic has referred to this scene as "grotesque,"[76] but this great attention to the little things in life, an ability to enjoy them and to be grateful for them, Zhivago shares with his author, who comes to reject the gigantic and the extraordinary and praises the natural limitations of man: "I do not trust anything that is too big or of which there is too much. Women bear people, not Cyclopes. Only inorganic phenomena are gigantic: the cosmic spaces of non-existence, the void of death, the deadening principles of deformity and vilification."[77]

The source of the ultimate failure of Antipov-Strelnikov is his search for heroic deeds combined with a disdain for simple human emotions. His preoccupation with generalizations causes him to overlook life itself. The art of Pushkin and Chekhov is especially appealing to Zhivago because of their disregard for the "ultimate aims of mankind." Their art becomes more meaningful as time goes by, precisely because they viewed it as their personal concern; by being interested in simple things, they touched upon the ultimate.[78]

A concern with his own life is not only an artist's right but his duty. As early as 1927 Pasternak spoke of the artist's own life and experience both as a logical and the most productive starting point for his art. It is a common characteristic of great realists that they consider their own life as an instrument for knowledge of life in general.[79]

One perceptive observer has suggested as an explanation of the ambiguity of Pasternak's course of action in Soviet society his organic inability "to take a position of hostility towards the world around him."[80] Perhaps this quality was at least partiall y esponsible for Anna Akhmatova's enigmatic characterization of Pasternak as a "divine hypocrite" (божественный лицемер).[81]

[76] Mark Višnjak, "Čelovek v istorii," *Vozdušnye Puti*, 1 (1960), p. 191.
[77] "Kraj, stavšij...," *op.cit.*, p. 183.
[78] *Sočinenija*, IV, 294.
[79] *Ibid.*, III, 160, 172.
[80] Ruge, "A Visit to Pasternak," *op.cit.*, p. 25.
[81] Axmatova, *op.cit.*, II, 342.

In his consistent emphasis on joy (the theme of the joy of existence in his work, his joyous response to people personally and through correspondence) Pasternak approaches the tradition of a great Russian mystic, St. Seraphim of Sarov (1759–1833). In broaching the subject of Pasternak's Christianity we must keep in mind that he was not a theologian, but a poet, and consequently was using language as a poet and not as a theologian. An analysis of Pasternak's novel from the point of view of the author's deviations from the dogma of the Orthodox Church can hardly prove valuable simply because *Doctor Zhivago* is not a theological work.[82]

The approach that emphasizes the existential nature of Pasternak's Christianity and traces its manifestations in his life and work—such as, for instance, Thomas Merton's interpretation in his "The Pasternak Affair"—is both more legitimate and successful.[83] The reality of the poet's religious experience can hardly be denied. It is clearly evident in the novel and in the poems of Zhivago, where Christian themes and imagery are very prominent and explicit. In *When the Weather Clears* there are no poems with overtly Christian thematics, but the poet's religious experience is all-pervasive. In the title poem of the book, a description of nature evokes in the poet the feeling of triumphant and, at the same time, humble joy: the whole world is seen as a cathedral and life as a long service that the poet attends with tears of joy.[84] In the poem "В больнице" ("In the Hospital"), the gravely ill poet thinks of approaching death and is filled with gratitude—he

---

[82] Sergej Levickij in his article about *Doktor Živago*, "Svoboda i bessmertie," *Mosty*, 2 (1959), pp. 224–36, touches upon this problem. D. V. Konstantinov ("'Doktor Živago' i bogoiskatel'stvo v SSSR," *Vestnik Instituta po Izučeniju SSSR* [München], 2 [April-June 1959], pp. 75–86) speaks about Pasternak's religious views in *Doktor Živago* as a reflection of the God-seeking of Soviet intellectuals; according to the author, these views are only pointing in the direction of Eastern Orthodox Christianity.

[83] Thomas Merton, "The Pasternak Affair," *Disputed Questions* (The New American Library, 1965), pp. 15–61.

[84] *Sočinenija*, III, 73.

experiences his life as a gift of God.[85] There is a letter that describes the same situation as this poem. In it more details are given, but the fundamental feeling of joy and gratitude is even stronger. Describing his condition and his emotions, the poet ends: "And I exulted and cried for happiness."[86]

In terms of Pasternak's biography, the religious themes of his late work have to be viewed as a return to, rather than as a discovery of, Christianity. In the poem "Dawn" (*Doctor Zhivago*), this is stated quite explicitly:

Ты значил все в моей судьбе.
Потом пришла война, разруха
И долго-долго о тебе
Ни слуху не было, ни духу.

И через много-много лет
Твой голос вновь меня встревожил.
Всю ночь читал я твой завет
И как от обморока ожил.[87]

You meant everything in my destiny.
Then came the war, the destruction,
And for a long, long time
Nothing was heard from you.

And many, many years later,
Your voice aroused me again.
I read your testament all night,
And I felt as if come back to life.

The supposition that the "I" of the poem refers not only to Zhivago but to Pasternak as well is supported by one of Pasternak's letters to Jacqueline de Proyart, in which he designates the years 1910–1912 as the period when his spiritual world was most intensely Christian.[88] In Pasternak's early books there are poems where religious motifs are unmistakable,

[85] *Ibid.*, III, 87.
[86] "Kraj, stavšij...," p. 194.
[87] *Sočinenija*, IV, 557.
[88] Proyart, *op.cit.*, p. 41.

but the ambiguity of expression and the complexity of imagery make those instances rather easy to overlook.[89] In the same letter he explains that Christianity always remained a source of extraordinary inspiration and a vital force in his life precisely because, although christened as an infant, he was not brought up in the Christian tradition and therefore his Christianity never had any traditional or institutional connections.

It has been suggested by Victor Frank—without any attempt to treat the poet as a mystic in the technical sense of the word— that by perceiving natural phenomena as an expression of spiritual energy, the poet approaches a mystic's experience of the penetration of the spiritual principle into our empirical reality.[90] Essentially, this is the position from which a parallel between Pasternak's Christianity and the personality and the teachings of St. Seraphim is drawn.

Canonized by the Russian Orthodox Church in 1903, St. Seraphim had a significant influence on the Russian religious renaissance of the twentieth century. He was seen as the harbinger of a new form of spirituality, which was to supplant the traditional forms, especially that of ascetical monasticism.[91] St. Seraphim's teaching was one of joy; he dressed in white instead of the traditional monastic black, greeted his visitors all year around with the paschal greeting "Christ is risen," and addressed everyone as "my joy."

St. Seraphim taught that the true aim of Christian life was in the acquisition of the Holy Spirit. The means of achieving this goal—accessible to every Christian—were seen not so much in the ascetic exercise (St. Seraphim's rule for the daily prayer for laymen—from the point of view of the Eastern Orthodox

[89] For example, such poems as "Davaj ronjat' slova" ("Let us drop words," My Sister, Life) and "Ballada" ("A Ballad," Above the Barriers, 1929).
[90] Viktor Frank, "Vodjanoj znak," Sbornik statej, posvjaščennyx..., p. 242.
[91] G. P. Fedotov, ed., A Treasury of Russian Spirituality (New York: Harper Torchbooks, n.d.), pp. 242–79. A complete source of information on St. Seraphim and his writings is a book by V. N. Il'in, Prepodobnyj Serafim Sarovskij (Paris: YMCA Press, 1930).

tradition—is surprisingly short and simple) as in an individual's creative effort. St. Seraphim visualized the transformation of man through his activity. A striking element of his teaching was the emphasis on the possibility of attaining the Holy Spirit under the normal conditions of the everyday life of a layman. This aspect was of particular appeal to twentieth century Russian religious thought.

Pasternak's statement about his religious beliefs in the letter to Jacqueline de Proyart that was mentioned earlier is very much in the spirit of St. Seraphim. Pasternak writes that he invariably disappoints those who question him about his religious views and opinions, because his approach is different from "discussions" about one's beliefs: "Une 'opinion' sur le Saint-Esprit ne vaut rien auprès de sa propre présence dans une oeuvre d'art."[92]

In the poem "August" (*Doctor Zhivago*), in the form of a dream, a prophetic vision of the poet's own funeral is presented.[93] There are many factual allusions to the circumstances of his life, and the setting is easily recognized as the cemetery at Peredelkino, where the poet was to be buried a few years later. His friends, present at the funeral, hear the dead poet's voice taking leave of his art and of his life. It is stressed that his voice is "physically perceivable." What appears to be of special significance is the date on which the funeral is placed. It is the sixth of August (old style), the feast of the Transfiguration. This fact is casually mentioned by someone who is present. After the date is established, the poet goes on to explain the meaning of Transfiguration in the Eastern Church:

[92] Proyart, *op.cit.*, p. 41.

[93] The theme of the poet's own death is generally not an uncommon one in poetry. Perhaps the best-known example in Russian poetry is Lermontov's poem "Son"; it is also a prominent theme in the poetry of both Innokentij Annenskij and Nikolaj Gumilev. Some prophetic element is present in all those instances: Lermontov's poet is shot in the Caucasus, as shortly afterwards was Lermontov himself; Gumilev repeatedly writes of his own violent death—he was shot by the Cheka; in Annenskij the theme of death is very often connected with suffocation and lack of air—he died of a heart attack.

Обыкновенно свет без пламени
Исходит в этот день с Фавора,
И осень, ясная как знаменье,
К себе приковывает взоры.[94]

Habitually, light without flame
Emanates from Mount Tabor on this day,
And autumn, clear as an omen,
Draws all eyes to itself.

"Light without flame" points to a mystical tradition of the Eastern Church, in which the light beheld by the apostles on Mount Tabor is understood, not metaphorically but realistically, as a manifestation of divine energy *perceived physically* by human eyes.[95] This particular aspect of the Eastern Orthodox mystical tradition forms the basis of St. Seraphim's teachings. As taught by St. Seraphim, the presence of the Holy Spirit is manifested as a physically perceivable transfiguration of man.

The connection of Pasternak's poem with this tradition is emphasized by his concentration on the poet's visual perception. The poet takes leave of "the azure and gold of Transfiguration": "Прощай, лазурь преображенская / И золото второго Спаса." On a literary plane, these colors point to the poetry of Bely and Blok, symbolists who were influenced by the poetry of Vladimir Soloviev. At the same time, just as the explanation of the essence of Transfiguration is followed by a very precise visual depiction of an autumnal day, azure and gold describe very accurately the coloring of late August (19, new style) in central Russia.

Pasternak's joyous acceptance of life does not imply, however, that he was not aware of the tragic aspects of human

[94] *Sočinenija*, IV, 549.

[95] This tradition owes its elaboration to the fourteenth-century Byzantine theologian, St. Gregory Palamas. See John Meyendorff, *A Study of Gregory Palamas* (London and New York: The Faith Press, 1964). For St. Seraphim's connections with this tradition see Vladimir Lossky, *The Mystical Theology of the Eastern Church* (Cambridge and London, 1968), Chapter 11, "The Divine Light," pp. 217–35.

existence. The times in which he lived had more than their share of human tragedy and suffering. It would be wrong to assume that Pasternak was untouched by it. His account of the impact the tragic deaths of Yashvili, Tabidze, and Tsvetaeva had on him is one example. Eschatological and tragic motifs are overshadowed in Pasternak's world view and work by his joyous acceptance of life, because, irrespective of external circumstances, man is always in possession of the supreme values: an ability to love and to be creative.

What helped Pasternak to retain his joy of existence and to survive, perhaps, both physically and spiritually, was his dedication to his work. For him work was both the meaning and the justification of the poet's life. He once spoke of work as being "more intelligent and more noble than man."[96]

Afinogenov has left interesting comments on Pasternak's attitude toward work. The entries in his diary pertinent to the subject were made in September 1937. Afinogenov, a considerably younger man than Pasternak, was overwhelmed by the latter's dedication to his work. Everything else, writes Afinogenov, was of secondary importance to him. He was surprised that Pasternak did not care to read newspapers, but had to admit that he never wasted any time: "He is always occupied with his work, books, himself.... And whether he found himself in a palace or in a prison cell—all the same he would be occupied and perhaps even more than here—at least he would not have to think about money and [various] concerns."[97] Afinogenov sensed that Pasternak's dedication to his work was not simply a result of his isolated life in Peredelkino but that it had deeper roots.

Pasternak's advice to Afinogenov—who had just lost his membership in the party and in the Union of Writers and was expecting arrest any day—was to work: "And this better time will come very soon—when you will become completely engrossed in your work, will begin to write and will forget

---

[96] *Sočinenija*, III, 159.
[97] Afinogenov, *op.cit.*, p. 153. See also p. 150.

about everything else."[98] Pasternak's attitude toward work should not be considered an escape from reality, even if it did have a therapeutic effect on him of which he was aware. Work is a cure for all because this is what an artist should be doing; for Pasternak, writing is a most natural occupation. Just as instead of discussing religion, the poet conveys the reality of his experience through his poetry, so instead of commenting on art, he produces works of art. In a poem written in 1921, discussions about art blend with discussions about transportation to produce the "grey crust" which envelops the poets and life itself.[99] A poet can justify his existence only by his work, by writing rather than by discussing art.

In the fifties the need to work becomes almost an obsession with Pasternak. His letters of the early fifties, before the publication of *Doctor Zhivago*, are full of references to work. He feels well because he is able to work a lot. Man's only concern should be his work: "It seems to me that all the efforts of man should be concentrated on his activity—successful, daring, and productive—and the rest will be accomplished by life."[100] He expresses joy that he has had to work all his life.[101] Work is an organic part of his life; he cannot live any other way: "I am used to have my every day filled with work, the way it is filled with the sun in the sky."[102] Work remains an effective antidote to loneliness and depression: "On those not infrequent days when autumn breathes darkness, cold, and loneliness into my face, I vanquish those fits of depression by our only salvation—work."[103]

Pasternak believed that the world-wide recognition of his last years increased his responsibility and therefore obliged him to work more intensely so as to justify the trust of his readers. But his letters of the late fifties are full of references to

[98] *Ibid.*
[99] *Sočinenija*, I, 86.
[100] "Kraj, stavšij...," *op.cit.*, p. 185.
[101] "Pis'ma druz'jam," *LG*, No. 2 (1966), p. 90.
[102] *Ibid.*, p. 91.
[103] *Ibid.*, pp. 92–93.

his desire and inability to work, probably largely because his lively correspondence with the West, which brought him something he had lacked for many years—the joy of communion with his audience—the difficulties at home that resulted from the publication of *Doctor Zhivago*, and last but not least, the necessity to earn his living, which became increasingly difficult after he was expelled from the Writers' Union in 1958 kept him from his work on the drama in prose, "Слепая красавица" ("Blind Beauty").[104]

An anonymous article in the *Times Literary Supplement*[105] very correctly pointed out Pasternak's jubilant acceptance of life as the manifest commitment of his most famous early book of verse, *My Sister, Life*. This affirmative and joyous attitude stood out both against the background of postwar Europe (the book was published in 1922) and of post-revolutionary Russia. The prime cause of the poet's exultation was not the revolutionary upheaval but a purely existential experience of living—an experience accessible to man in all ages.

Surveying Pasternak's art and career, one comes to the conclusion that through the long years of his life he remained faithful to his commitment to Life, which he served through his art. Once the poet found his true vocation, what remained for him was to fulfill it—and he did it by working incessantly till his death.

---

[104] Ruge, *op.cit.*, p. 23; Schweitzer, *op.cit.*, p. 79, 104, see also pp. 60 and 111; Merton, *op.cit.*, pp. 218–19.
[105] "Zhivago's Defence," *Times Literary Supplement*, March 11, 1965.

CONCLUSION

IT HAS been repeatedly and convincingly suggested that Pasternak has an affinity with romanticism. Specific links between his poetry and certain features of the poetry of the Russian romantics—Lermontov, Tyutchev, and Fet—have been pointed out.[1] On the other hand, it has been asserted—on the basis of other specific peculiarities of his poetry—that Pasternak is not a romantic.[2] One has to admit that both views

[1] Gleb Struve speaks of Pasternak's "kinship with the romantic tradition in Russian poetry" as being "beyond question." Struve points out that Pasternak shares Lermontov's passionate intensity and Tjutčev's intense cosmic feeling (*Russian Literature under Lenin and Stalin*, p. 182). Jurij Tynjanov suggests a relationship with Fet ("Promežutok," *Arxaisty i novatory*, pp. 562–68). Even a superficial glance at Pasternak's epigraphs and dedications reveals his strong affinity with the romantic poets (see Vera Aleksandrova, "Po literaturnym adresam poèta," *Vozdušnye Puti*, 1 [1960], pp. 118–34). There have been attempts to treat Pasternak's "romanticism" as a perpetuation and a direct offspring of romantic aesthetics of the nineteenth century. See, for instance, Guy de Mallac, "Zur Ästhetik Pasternaks," *Sowjet Studien*, No. 16 (June, 1964), pp. 78–101; Victor Terras, "Boris Pasternak and Romantic Aesthetics," *Papers on Language and Literature*, III, No. 1 (Winter 1967), pp. 42–56.

[2] Z. Papernyj, "B. L. Pasternak," in *Istorija russkoj sovetskoj literatury* (2nd ed.; 4 vols.; Moskva: Nauka, 1968), III, 350–88. As the reason for the conclusion that Pasternak was not a romantic is mentioned his sharpness of vision, which would not allow the poet to be satisfied with "romantic haze, diffusiveness, devotion to the exceptional, and disregard for the everyday" (p. 372). This statement is true in so far as the specific qualities are concerned, but erroneous in reducing romanticism to the qualities listed.

168

are essentially true. There are some elements of Pasternak's poetics that place him within romanticism, and there are others, equally strong and indisputable, that belie this relationship.

It is highly characteristic of Pasternak that—after his early and short-lived participation in the futurist Centrifuge—he very consistently avoided associating himself not only with contemporary literary organizations and trends but also with literary movements in a broader sense. His abhorrence of labels and classifications stemmed from a conviction that they never tell the whole truth. This is especially true in Pasternak's case: a poet as original and as complex as he, who lived to be seventy and continued writing until his death, can hardly fit any standard category.

When describing the romantic hero worship that he had rejected early in his career, Pasternak quite correctly identified it as a by-product of the romantic world view transmitted to the poets of his generation through the symbolists, who, in their turn, inherited it from the German romantics. In describing the origin of something he had rejected, Pasternak was actually revealing the genealogy of his own poetics.

Pasternak shared the basic tenets of romantic aesthetics: for him art was a means of cognition of the world; the organic unity of the cosmos and man's part in it were a tangible reality for the poet. Art, in Pasternak's view, was not engaged in imitating nature but rather in continuing its creative work.

Among Russian symbolists, Blok and Skryabin were most influential for Pasternak's formative period. The elements of Skryabin's world view—his influence was the earliest and perhaps the strongest—that had the greatest impact on the young Pasternak were the belief in the transforming powers of art and in the exceptional role assigned to the creative artist.

But it has to be remembered that one of the fundamental characteristics of Pasternak's personality was the extreme selectivity of approach. Romantic hero worship Pasternak rejected as a very young man. Despite the importance he continued to attach to the role of the creative artist, he was

169

invariably suspicious of those views which conceivably might have led to a dramatization of the poet's life. The romantic view of the significance of an individual took a Christian turn in his world view. Pasternak went further than just asserting the value of every individual: his poet cannot exist without other people. Pasternak's aversion to "organizations" and "societies" reflects his strong anti-utopian convictions. His mistrust of collective actions, which, as he was to remark, without exception are tinged with hysteria,[3] only strengthened his faith in the individual. As one of the poet's goals Pasternak saw his creative influence on his time—"not openly, not collectively, but internally and invisibly."[4]

The belief in the transforming powers of art remained one of the cornerstones of Pasternak's poetics. His view differed from that of the symbolists, however, in that for Pasternak it was not a potential that would be realized in the art of the future, nor, as the forerunner of Russian symbolists, Vladimir Soloviev, believed, at the end of history; this power is realized here and now, in every true work of art. It is absolutely impossible to associate Pasternak—even the early Pasternak—with something like Skryabin's plans and preparations for the realization of his *Mysterium*, in a temple that was to be erected specially for the occasion in India!

Romantic hero worship was not the only feature of romanticism that had no place in Pasternak's poetics. The realm of the fantastic held no appeal for the poet, for he was able to perceive the exceptional in the most ordinary and in the everyday. In 1959, questioned on the subject of romanticism by one of his Western correspondents, Pasternak wrote that his negative attitude was not toward the romantic movement, but to "romanticism as a principle," that is, to everything in art— irrespective of the period or school—that is not original, but secondary and derivative, to "literature about literature." Rejecting this kind of romanticism, which implies an artist's

---

[3] Hélène Zamoyska, "L'art et la vie chez Boris Pasternak," *Revue des études slaves* (Mèlanges Pierre Pascal), 38 (1961), pp. 238–39.

[4] Schweitzer, *op.cit.*, p. 15.

admiration of his own art and serving art through his art, Pasternak suggests—admitting that he exaggerates—that the true artist serves and worships life by means of his art, but looks almost with contempt at his own art as such.[5] From a careful examination of Pasternak's views on art and of their application in his work there emerges a picture of fundamental unity and continuity. The essentials of his poetics and his world view were worked out and made public relatively early. "A Few Principles," an article published in 1922, can be considered a summary of the poet's views.[6] The basic premises expounded in this article were not new to Pasternak at the time of its writing, nor were they abandoned later: Safe Conduct and many later pronouncements reiterate the same views.

In "A Few Principles" the poet's total commitment to art is stressed; it is opposed both to the amateurishly superficial interest in art and to a purely theoretical approach to it. The view of art as play is ruled out altogether; Pasternak's extremely serious and responsible attitude toward art is akin to Blok's. Many years later, in a private letter Pasternak was to recall Tolstoy's contrast between Vronsky's and Anna's dabbling in art as a pleasant pastime and a poor painter's life commitment to and obsession with art. His own devotion to art Pasternak compared to the totality of religious belief.[7]

Because of its unpredictability, poetry is spoken of in "A Few Principles" as a dangerous entity: it is something beyond and outside logic. However, the only demand that Pasternak places directly on the writer is the preservation of life's voice in his art. For in its connection with and its dependence on life is the source of art's actuality. Its sole claim to significance is that it is a corollary of life, with no beginning or end.

A spontaneity and an inspiration that are akin to intoxication are permanent ingredients of Pasternak's art. In his early works he is apt to speak about them directly; later their presence—although unannounced—remains unmistakable. But

[5] Ibid., pp. 80–81, 89.
[6] Sočinenija, III, 152–55.
[7] "Kraj, stavšij...," op.cit., pp. 196 and 182.

171

the all-pervasive emotional intensity of Pasternak's poetry does not eliminate order from his poetic world. Spontaneous emotion is at all times counterbalanced by a quest for order.[8] Pasternak's lifelong striving to overcome the complexity of his poetic manner—which was certainly not a lack of order, but was perhaps an order too complex—stemmed from a desire to attain a more easily perceivable order. His search for simplicity was not a betrayal of a desire—common to post-symbolist poets—to convey a poet's experience in all its complexity but an attempt to make that complexity more accessible. The difference between his early and late manner of expression Pasternak compared to being *incomprehensibly* and *comprehensibly* true.[9] The key word here—in keeping with the ideas expressed in "A Few Principles"—is "true."

There was no question in Pasternak's mind that the creative process had to be in direct contact with reality. His criticism of the over-refined art of the early twentieth century—whose descendant he felt himself to be—was that it was a spirituality that lacked contact with actuality; he compared it to "unused light," light from which no one benefits.[10] An artist has to respond creatively to his time: he has to change with the changing times. In his desire to keep in step with contemporary developments, Pasternak renounced many things that were a part of his life before the Revolution. Very consciously, he did not search for answers in the past, and he accepted the actuality, but on the condition of preserving his integrity.

Pasternak's poetics can be described as aesthetic realism. He rejected both aestheticism and the utilitarian approach to art. Art for him was an objective reality; he shared the modern outlook that poetry has a purpose of its own, which it achieves by its own means. Pasternak's concept of realism presupposes a never-ending fascination with everyday existence, but it does not eliminate spiritual values from his conception of life and art and therefore, in essence, is not related to nineteenth-century positivism and its perpetuation in our time.

---

[8] An early poem "Piry" (*Sočinenija*, I, 184) develops the juxtaposition of spontaneity and order with almost programmatic directness.

[9] Schweitzer, *op.cit.*, p. 87.   [10] *Ibid.*, p. 49.

In his nontraditional usage of the term "realism," Pasternak follows Blok, who in 1919 spoke of true realism as not imitating but transforming nature, and thus being a legitimate heir to romanticism, which is not a rejection of life but a new vision and a more intense experience of life, the "sixth sense" of mankind.[11] Pasternak's realism fits what has been described as the "imaginative realism" of post-symbolist poetry, with its desire to enter into all spheres of existence and to be minutely precise in its depiction of the poet's complex experiences and impressions.[12]

In one of Pasternak's last poems, "Зимние праздники" ("Winter Holidays," 1959), the essence of his poetics is clearly presented:

Будущего недостаточно,
Старого, нового мало.
Надо, чтоб елкою святочной
Вечность средь комнаты стала.[13]

The future is not sufficient,
The old and the new are not enough.
It is necessary that—like a Christmas tree—
Eternity stand in the middle of the room.

This is not a dismissal of the past or the future, but it is an uncompromising demand for eternity to transcend time—to be manifest in the present. Eternity—as festive and as modest as a Christmas tree—enters the poet's room; in Pasternak's poetic world, this is not an extraordinary development but an everyday occurrence. This maximum demand placed on art and on man's spiritual powers is equally typical of Pasternak the young poet of the pre-revolutionary years and of the Nobel prize winner of 1958.

[11] Aleksandr Blok, "O romantizme," *Sobranie sočinenij*, VI, 359–71. The correspondence between Pasternak's views and those of Blok was brought to my attention by an article of H. Zamoyska ("L'art et la vie chez Boris Pasternak," *op.cit.*, pp. 231–39).

[12] C. M. Bowra, *The Creative Experiment* (New York: Grove Press, n.d.), p. 10.

[13] *Sočinenija*, III, 106.

BIBLIOGRAPHY

THE WORKS listed here appear in the text or in the footnotes. They are assigned to one of the following categories: works by Pasternak, critical and memoir literature about Pasternak, general works not specifically concerned with Pasternak.

PART I

The three-volume Michigan edition of Boris Pasternak's works, edited by Gleb Struve and Boris Filippov (Ann Arbor: The University of Michigan Press, 1961), was used throughout the text as the basic edition of Pasternak's works. Boris Pasternak's critical essays and speeches published in various periodicals were not collected during his lifetime. Neither has his autobiographical or fictional prose been republished since the thirties. The Michigan edition is the first attempt at "collected works"; as such it greatly facilitated my work.

In the notes, the Michigan edition is referred to as *Sočinenija*. The volumes are numbered as follows:

Volume I: *Stixi i poèmy 1912–1932.*

Volume II: *Proza 1915–1958. Povesti, rasskazy, avtobiografičeskie proizvedenija.*

Volume III: *Stixi 1936–1959. Stixi dlja detej. Stixi 1912–1957, ne sobrannye v knigi avtora. Stat'i i vystuplenija.*

The University of Michigan Press edition of *Doktor Živago* (1959) is designated Volume IV of *Sočinenija*.

175

The 1965 volume of Pasternak's poetry (*Stixotvorenija i poèmy. Biblioteka poèta, Bol'šaja serija* [Moskva-Leningrad: Sovetskij pisatel']) was used for those early poems and the variants which were not available in the West before and thus were not included in the Michigan edition.

The following list includes those works, letters, and translations of Pasternak's which are not found either in *Sočinenija* or *Stixotvorenija*, and which are cited in the text or in the notes.

Section A

The Blind Beauty. Translated by Manya Harari and Max Hayward. New York: Harcourt, Brace & World, Inc., 1969. *Slepaja krasavica.* Original text. A limited edition by the same publisher.

"Boris Pasternak o sebe i o čitateljax," with comments by Gleb Struve. *Grani*, 53 (1963), pp. 76–79. Originally in *Čitatel' i Pisatel'*, February 11, 1928, Nos. 4–5. "Boris Pasternak about Himself and His Readers," translated by Gleb Struve. *Slavic Review*, XXIII, No. 1 (March 1964), pp. 125–28.

"Ljudi i položenija." *Novyj Mir*, No. 1 (1967), pp. 204–36. Except for minor changes and understandable deletions, reproduces the text of *Avtobiografičeskij očerk*.

"Slovo o poèzii." A speech delivered in June 1935 at the International Congress of Writers for the Defense of Culture in Paris. Published with comments by Gleb Struve in *Sbornik statej, posvjaščennyx tvorčestvu B. L. Pasternaka*. München, 1962. Pp. 9–15.

"Vassermanova reakcija." *Rukonog*, Sbornik stixov i kritiki. Moskva: Centrifuga, 1914. Pp. 33–38.

"Vladimir Majakovskij. *Prostoe, kak myčanie.*" Published together with "Zametki perevodčika" and "Šopen" under the title "Kritičeskie ètjudy" in *Literaturnaja Rossija*, March 19, 1965, pp. 18–19, with an introductory note by Evgenij Pasternak.

Section B

"Čudo poètičeskogo vploščenija" (Pis'ma Borisa Pasternaka). *Voprosy Literatury*, No. 9 (1972), pp. 139–71. Eighteen letters written between 1912 and 1956.

Letters to Maksim Gor'kij (1921, 1927–1928). Published in *Literaturnoe Nasledstvo* (Gor'kij i sovetskie pisateli), 70 (1963), pp. 295–310.

Letter to Rainer Maria Rilke. Published in Marina Cvetaeva. *Nesobrannye proizvedenija* ("Ausgewählte Werke"), ed. Günther Wytrzens, München: Wilhelm Fink Verlag, 1971. Pp. 681–83.

Letter to Vjačeslav Polonskij (June 1, 1927). *Novyj Mir*, No. 10 (1964), pp. 195–96.

"Pis'ma druz'jam" (1931–1959). *Literaturnaja Gruzija*, No. 1 (1966), pp. 75–91, and No. 2 (1966), pp. 83–96.

"Nine Letters of Boris Pasternak," letters to Pasternak's English translator, George Reavey (1931–1933, 1943, 1959–1960). Translated and annotated by Elena Levin. *Harvard Library Bulletin*, xv, No. 4 (October 1967), pp. 317–30.

"Kraj, stavšij mne vtoroj rodinoj" (Pis'ma B. Pasternaka k gruzinskim pisateljam) (1932–1959). *Voprosy Literatury*, No. 1 (1966), pp. 166–200.

Three letters of Boris Pasternak to Tician Tabidze (1933–1935). Tabidze, Tician. *Stat'i, očerki, perepiska.* Tbilisi, 1964. Pp. 246–51.

Letter to Josef Hóra (November 15, 1935). Published in the Czech translation of *Oxrannaja gramota: Glejt.* Praha: Státní nakladatelství krásné literatury a umění, 1965. The letter is printed between pp. 182 and 183.

Letter to Tamara Jašvili (August 28, 1937). *Literaturnaja Gruzija*, No. 7 (1964), pp. 88–89.

Letter to Mrs. Beatrice Nosco (May 5, 1959). Unpublished.

"Three Letters to Stephen Spender" (August–September 1959). *Encounter*, 83 (August, 1960), pp. 3–6.

BIBLIOGRAPHY

Letter to Thomas Merton (February 7, 1960). Published in Merton, Thomas. *Disputed Questions*. New York: The New American Library, 1965. Pp. 218–19.

Section C

Ril'ke, Rajner Marija. "Rekviem." Translated by B. Pasternak. *Zvezda*, No. 8 (1929), pp. 167–70.

———. "Po odnoj podruge Rekviem." Translated by B. Pasternak. *Novyj Mir*, Nos. 8–9 (1929), pp. 63–69.

PART II

Aleksandrov, V. "Častnaja žizn'." *Literaturnyj Kritik*, 3 (1937), pp. 55–81.

Aleksandrova, Vera. "Po literaturnym adresam poèta." *Vozdušnye Puti* (New York), 1 (1960), pp. 118–34.

Aucouturier, Michel. "Il Tratto di Apelle. Manifeste littéraire du modernisme russe." *Revue des études slaves*, XLVII (1968), pp. 157–61.

"B. Pasternak i Sojuz Sov[etskix] Pisatelej" (Stenogramma). *Novyj Žurnal*, 83 (1966), pp. 185–227.

Berlin, Isaiah. "The Energy of Pasternak." *Partisan Review* (1950), pp. 748–51.

Bowra, C. M. "Boris Pasternak, 1917–1923." *The Creative Experiment*. New York: Grove Press, n.d. Pp. 128–58.

Carlisle, Olga. "Three Visits with Boris Pasternak." *The Paris Review*, 24 (Summer-Fall 1960), pp. 45–69.

Conquest, Robert. *The Pasternak Affair: Courage of Genius.* Philadelphia and New York: J. B. Lippincott, 1962.

Čukovskij, Kornej. "I obraz mira, v slove javlennyj ..." *Junost'*, No. 8 (1965), pp. 66–70.

Cvetaeva, Marina. "Èpos i lirika sovremennoj Rossii— Vladimir Majakovskij i Boris Pasternak." *Novyj Grad* (Paris), Nos. 6 and 7 (1933), pp. 28–41, 66–80.

———. "Svetovoj liven'." *Proza*. New York: Chekhov Publishing House, 1953. Pp. 353–71.

Davie, Donald. *The Poems of Dr. Zhivago.* Manchester: Manchester University Press, 1965.

Frank, Victor, "A Russian Hamlet: Boris Pasternak's Novel." *The Dublin Review* (September 1958), pp. 212–20.

Frank, Viktor. "Vodjanoj znak" (Poètičeskoe mirovozzrenie Pasternaka), *Sbornik statej, posvjaščennyx tvorčestvu B. L. Pasternaka.* München, 1962. Pp. 240–52.

Jakobson, Roman. "Randbemerkungen zur Prosa des Dichters Pasternak." *Slavische Rundschau,* No. 6 (1935), pp. 357–74.

Konstantinov, D. V. "'Doktor Živago' i bogoiskatel'stvo v SSSR." *Vestnik Instituta po Izučeniju SSSR* (München), 2 (30) (April–June 1959), pp. 75–86.

Korjakov, Mixail. "Termometr Rossii." *Novyj Žurnal,* 55 (1958), pp. 130–41.

Letter to Boris Pasternak by the editorial board of *Novyj Mir* (September, 1956). *Novyj Mir,* No. 11 (1958), pp. iii–xvi.

Levickij, Sergej. "Svoboda i bessmertie." *Mosty,* 2 (1959), pp. 224–36.

Ležnev, A. "Boris Pasternak." *Sovremenniki.* Moskva: Krug, 1927. Pp. 32–54.

Mallac, Guy de. "Zur Ästhetik Pasternaks." *Sowjet Studien* (Institut zur Erforschung des UdSSR), No. 16 (June 1964), pp. 78–101.

"A Man Alone." *Manchester Guardian* (November 6, 1958), p. 1.

Markov, Vladimir. "An Unnoticed Aspect of Pasternak's Translations." *Slavic Review,* xx, No. 3 (October 1961), pp. 503–08.

Matlaw, Ralph. "A Visit with Pasternak." *Nation* (September 12, 1959), pp. 134–35.

Merton, Thomas. "The Pasternak Affair." *Disputed Questions.* New York: The New American Library, 1965. Pp. 15–61.

Miller-Budnickaja, R. "O 'filosofii iskusstva' B. Pasternaka i R. M. Ril'ke." *Zvezda,* No. 5 (1932), pp. 160–68.

Mirskij, D. "Pasternak i gruzinskie poèty." *Literaturnaja Gazeta,* October 24, 1935.

Muchnic, Helen. "Boris Pasternak and the Poems of Yurii

Zhivago." *From Gorky to Pasternak.* New York: Random House, 1961. Pp. 341–404.

Nilsson, Nils Åke. "Besuch bei Boris Pasternak. September 1958." *Boris Pasternak. Bescheidenheit und Kühnheit.* Zürich, 1959. Pp. 102–13.

Oblomievskij, D. "Boris Pasternak." *Literaturnyj Sovremennik,* 4 (1934), pp. 127–42.

Obolenskij, D. D. "Stixi Doktora Živago." *Sbornik statej, posvjaščennyx tvorčestvu B. L. Pasternaka.* München, 1962. Pp. 103–14.

Papernyj, Z. "B. L. Pasternak." *Istorija russkoj sovetskoj literatury.* 4 vols. Moskva: Nauka. Second edition. III (1968), pp. 350–88.

Peltier-Zamoyska, Hélène. "Pasternak, homme du passé?" *Esprit,* XXXI, No. 1 (January 1963), pp. 16–29.

Pravduxin, Valerian. "V bor'be za novoe iskusstvo." *Sibirskie Ogni,* No. 5 (1922), pp. 174–81.

Proyart, Jacqueline de. *Pasternak.* Paris: Gallimard, 1964.

Raevsky-Hughes, Olga. "Boris Pasternak i Marina Cvetaeva (K istorii družby)." *Vestnik Russkogo Studenčeskogo Xristianskogo Dviženija* (Paris), 100 (1971), pp. 281–305.

Rowland, Mary F., and Rowland, Paul. *Pasternak's Doctor Zhivago.* Carbondale: Southern Illinois University Press, 1967.

Ruge, Gerd. "A Visit to Pasternak." *Encounter,* 54 (March 1958), pp. 22–25.

Schweitzer, Renate. *Freundschaft mit Boris Pasternak: Ein Briefwechsel.* Verlag Kurt Desch, 1963.

Selivanovskij, A. "Poèzija opasna?" *Literaturnaja Gazeta,* August 15, 1931.

Sinjavskij, A. "Poèzija Pasternaka," an introductory article in Boris Pasternak, *Stixotvorenija i poèmy.* Biblioteka poèta, Bol'šaja serija. Moskva-Leningrad: Sovetskij Pisatel', 1965. Pp. 9–62.

Stepun, Fedor. "B. L. Pasternak." *Novyj Žurnal,* 56 (1959), pp. 187–206.

Struve, Gleb. "Sense and Nonsense about *Doctor Zhivago.*"

Studies in Russian and Polish Literatures in Honor of Wacław Lednicki. Edited by Z. Folejewski. Mouton, 1962. Pp. 229–50.

Terras, Victor. "Boris Pasternak and Romantic Aesthetics." *Papers on Language and Literature*, III, No. 1 (Winter 1967), pp. 42–56.

Tynjanov, Jurij. "Promežutok" (O poèzii), *Arxaisty i novatory.* Leningrad: Priboj, 1929. Pp. 541–80.

Višnjak, Mark. "Čelovek v istorii." *Vozdušnye Puti* (New York), 1 (1960), pp. 180–99.

Voznesenskij, Andrej. "Nebo Borisa Pasternaka." *Inostrannaja Literatura*, No. 1 (1968), pp. 199–203.

Wright-Kovaleva, R. "Vse lučšie vospominan'ja ..." *Oxford Slavonic Papers*, XIII (1967), pp. 108–32.

Zamoyska, Hélène. "L'art et la vie chez Boris Pasternak." *Revue des études slaves* (Mèlanges Pierre Pascal), XXXVIII (1961), pp. 231–39.

Zelinskij, Kornelij. "Liričeskaja tetrad'." *God Šestnadcatyj*, No. 1 (1933), pp. 391–407.

"Zhivago's Defence." *The Times Literary Supplement* (March 11, 1965), pp. 185–86.

PART III

Afinogenov, Aleksandr. *Stat'i, dnevniki, pis'ma, vospominanija.* Moskva: Iskusstvo, 1957.

Annenskij, Innokentij. "O sovremennom lirizme." *Apollon*, No. 1 (1909), pp. 12–42; No. 2 (1909), pp. 3–29.

Asaf'ev, Boris. *Skrjabin. Opyt xarakteristiki.* Peterburg-Berlin: Svetozar, 1923.

Axmatova, Anna. *Sočinenija.* 2 vols. Inter-Language Literary Associates, 1965, 1968.

Belyj, Andrej. "Magija slov." *Simvolizm.* Moskva: Musaget, 1910. Pp. 429–48.

Berdjaev, Nikolaj. "Personalizm i marksizm." *Put'* (Paris), 48 (1935), pp. 3–19.

BIBLIOGRAPHY

Blok, Aleksandr. "O sovremennom sostojanii russkogo simvolizma." *Apollon*, No. 8 (1910), pp. 21–30.
———. *Sobranie sočinenij v vos'mi tomax.* Moskva-Leningrad: GIXL, 1960.
Bowra, C. M. "The Creative Experiment." *The Creative Experiment.* New York: Grove Press, n.d. Pp. 1–28.
Brjusov, Valerij. "Karl V," Dialog o realizme v iskusstve. *Zolotoe Runo*, No. 4 (1906), pp. 61–67.
———. "Novye tečenija v russkoj poèzii." *Russkaja Mysl'*, No. 3 (1913), pp. 124–33.
"Brjusov—teoretik simvolizma" (K istorii simvolizma). Published with comments by K. Loks in *Literaturnoe Nasledstvo*, 27–28 (1937), pp. 269–75.
Buxarin, N. *Poèzija, poètika i zadači poètičeskogo tvorčestva v SSSR.* Moskva: GIXL, 1934.
Čukovskij, Kornej. "Ègo-futuristy i kubo-futuristy." *Šipovnik* (Peterburg), XXII (1914), pp. 97–135.
Elagin, Jurij. *Ukroščenie iskusstv.* New York: Chekhov Publishing House, 1952.
Evtušenko, Evgenij [Yevtushenko, Yevgeny]. *A Precocious Autobiography.* Translated by Andrew R. MacAndrew. New York: Dutton, 1964.
Èjxenbaum, Boris. "Sud'ba Bloka." *Skvoz' literaturu.* Mouton, 1962. Pp. 215–32.
Gofman, V. "Jazyk simvolistov." *Literaturnoe Nasledstvo*, 27–28 (1937), pp. 54–105.
Gumilev, Nikolaj. *Sobranie sočinenij v četyrex tomax.* Vol. II. Washington: Victor Kamkin, 1964.
Il'in, V. N. *Prepodobnyj Serafim Sarovskij.* Paris: YMCA Press, 1930.
Ivanov, Vjačeslav. "Poèt i čern'." *Po zvezdam.* Peterburg: Ory, 1909. Pp. 33–42.
———. "Zavety simvolizma." *Apollon*, No. 8 (1910), pp. 5–20.
Ivanov-Razumnik, R. V. *Vladimir Majakovskij ("Misterija" ili "Buff").* Berlin: Skify, 1922.
Kaverin, V. "Neskol'ko let." *Novyj Mir*, No. 11 (1966), pp. 132–58.

182

Leonard, Richard Anthony. *A History of Russian Music.* New York: The Macmillan Company, 1957.

Lossky, Vladimir. *The Mystical Theology of the Eastern Church.* Cambridge and London: James Clarke & Co., Ltd., 1968.

Mandel'štam, Nadežda. *Vospominanija.* New York: Chekhov Publishing House, 1970.

Mandel'štam, Osip. "Puškin i Skrjabin." *Sobranie sočinenij v trex tomax.* Edited by Gleb Struve and Boris Filippov. Inter-Language Literary Associates, 1967–1971, Vol. II. Pp. 313–19.

Markov, Vladimir. "Mysli o russkom futurizme." *Novyj Žurnal,* 38 (1954), 169–81.

————. *Russian Futurism: A History.* Berkeley and Los Angeles: University of California Press, 1968.

Meyendorff, John. *A Study of Gregory Palamas.* London and New York: The Faith Press, 1964.

"Pis'ma Mariny Cvetaevoj." Publikacija A. S. Èfron. *Novyj Mir,* No. 4 (1969), 185–214.

Priglušennye golosa. Edited by Vladimir Markov. New York: Chekhov Publishing House, 1952.

Rilke, Rainer Maria. *Gesammelte Gedichte.* Insel Verlag, 1962.

————. *Selected Works.* Vol. I: *Prose.* Translated by G. Craig Houston. London: The Hogarth Press, 1954.

Sabaneev, Leonid. *Modern Russian Composers.* Translated from the Russian by Judah A. Joffe. New York: International Publishers, 1927.

Struve, Gleb. *Russian Literature under Lenin and Stalin, 1917–1953.* Norman: University of Oklahoma Press, 1971.

Šlecer, B. F. *A. Skrjabin.* Vol. I. Berlin: Grani, 1923.

Taranovski, Kiril. "O vzaimootnošenii stixotvornogo ritma i tematiki." *American Contributions to the Fifth International Congress of Slavists.* Mouton, 1963. Vol. I, pp. 287–322.

A Treasury of Russian Spirituality. Edited by G. P. Fedotov. New York: Harper and Row, 1965.

Xodasevič, Vladislav. "O simvolizme." *Literaturnye stat'i i vospominanija.* New York: Chekhov Publishing House, 1954. Pp. 153–58.

INDEX

IN ADDITION to the names that occur in the text and in the footnotes, this index lists all the works of Pasternak (including individual poems) that are mentioned; names of fictional characters, as well as those of literary scholars and critics appearing in bibliographical references in the footnotes are omitted.

INDEX

When the Weather Clears, see *Kogda razguljaetsja*
"When the Weather Clears," see "Kogda razguljaetsja"
"Winter Holidays," see "Zimnie prazdniki"
"Xleb," 148
"Xudožnik," 60–61
"Year 1905, The," see "Devjat'sot pjatyj god"
"You are at hand, distant expanse of socialism," see "Ty rjadom, dal' socializma"
"You have a right, having turned your pocket inside out," see "Ty vprave, vyvernuv karman"
"Zamestitel'nica," 28–29
"Zametki k perevodam šekspirovskix tragedij," 20n
"Zarevo," 155–156
"Zdes' budet vse: perežitoe," 144
"Zemlja," 70, 71n
"Zimnie prazdniki," 173

Pasternak, Yevgeny, 130n
Peter the Great, 30, 92
Plato, 88–89
Proyart, Jacqueline de, 161, 163
Pushkin, Alexander, 11, 39–40, 49, 54, 62, 92, 99n, 108, 137, 159

Raykh, Z. N., 141–142
Rilke, Rainer Maria, 116, 126, 133, 139

Rodin, Auguste, 139
Rowland, Mary F., 74n
Rowland, Paul, 74n

Sabaneev, Leonid, 10n
Seraphim of Sarov, Saint, 160, 162–164
Shakespeare, William, 41, 146, 150n
Sinyavsky, Audrey, 31, 65
Skryabin, Alexander, 9–14, 55, 62, 132, 169–170
Soloviev, Vladimir, 164, 170
Stalin, Iosif, 81, 96, 102n–103n, 136, 150, 156, 157n
Struve, Gleb, 93, 168n
Swinburne, Algernon Charles, 40

Tabidze, Titian, 67, 151, 165
Taranovsky, Kiril, 54n
Tolstoy, Lev, 49, 63, 99, 103, 135, 171
Tsvetaeva, Marina, 36, 48, 105–106, 109–110, 151, 165
Tynyanov, Yury, 46, 49, 168n
Tyutchev, Fedor, 168

Verlaine, Paul Marie, 61, 62, 69

Wright-Kovaleva, Rita, 130–131n

Yashvili, Paolo, 115–116, 151, 165

Zamoyska, Hélène Peltier, 76n, 173n
Zinoviev, Grigory, 150n

PRINCETON ESSAYS IN LITERATURE

191

Library of Congress Cataloging in Publication Data

Hughes, Olga Raevsky.
The Poetic World of Boris Pasternak

(Princeton essays in European and comparative
Literature)
  Bibliography: p. 175
  1. Pasternak, Boris Leonidovich, 1890-1960.
I. Title.

PG3476.P27Z69   891.7'1'42   73-2467
ISBN 0-691-06262-5

192